WORCESTER, MASSACHUSETTS

"The Heart of the Commonwealth"

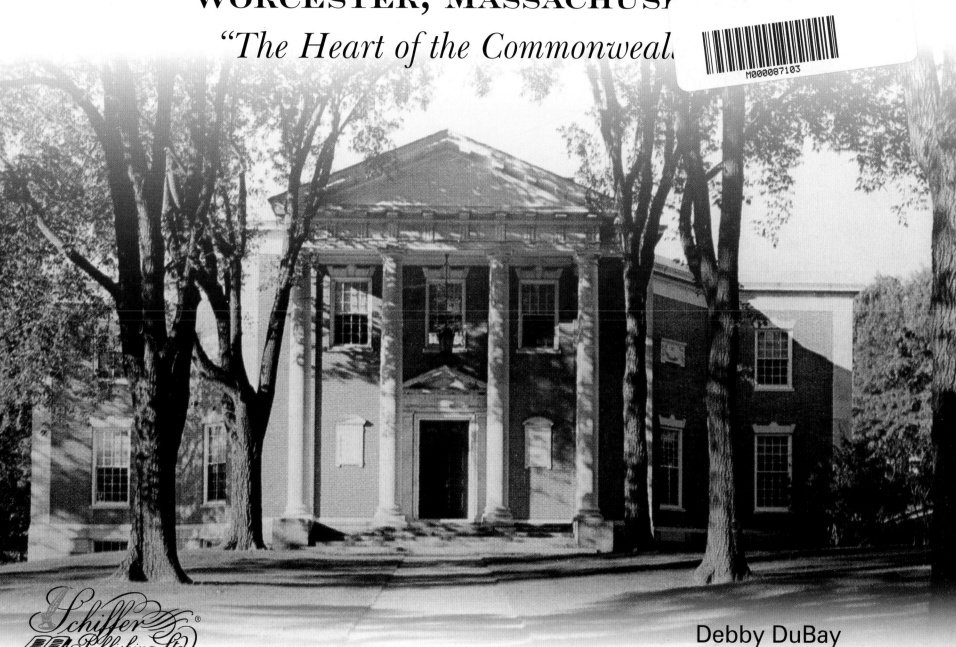

Debby DuBay

Schiffer Publishing Ltd

4880 Lower Valley Road Atglen, Pennsylvania 19310

Other Schiffer Books by Debby DuBay:

Antique Limoges at Home. ISBN:0-7643-1638-9. $49.95

Living with Limoges. ISBN: 0-7643-1451-3. $49.95

Collecting Hand Painted Limoges Porcelain. ISBN:0-7643-1886-1. $49.95

Beatrix Potter Collectibles: the Peter Rabbit Story Characters. with Kara Sewall. ISBN: 0-7643-2358-X. $29.95

Schiffer Books are available at special discounts for bulk purchases for sales promotions or premiums. Special editions, including personalized covers, corporate imprints, and excerpts can be created in large quantities for special needs. For more information contact the publisher:

Published by Schiffer Publishing Ltd.
4880 Lower Valley Road
Atglen, PA 19310
Phone: (610) 593-1777
Fax: (610) 593-2002
E-mail: Info@schifferbooks.com

For the largest selection of fine reference books on this and related subjects, please visit our web site at www.schifferbooks.com
We are always looking for people to write books on new and related subjects. If you have an idea for a book please contact us at the above address.

This book may be purchased from the publisher. Include $5.00 for shipping. Please try your bookstore first. You may write for a free catalog.

In Europe, Schiffer books are distributed by
Bushwood Books
6 Marksbury Ave.
Kew Gardens
Surrey TW9 4JF England
Phone: 44 (0) 20 8392-8585
Fax: 44 (0) 20 8392-9876
E-mail: info@bushwoodbooks.co.uk

Website: www.bushwoodbooks.co.uk
Free postage in the U.K., Europe; air mail at cost.

Designed by Stephanie Daugherty
Type set in Adobe Jenson Pro/ Zurich BT

ISBN: 978-0-7643-3138-1
Printed in China

Contents

Chapter 1
Introduction

Worcester (pronounced "wuster"), Massachusetts, nicknamed "The Heart of the Commonwealth," is *a city on the move.* Located in central Massachusetts, approximately 45 miles west of Boston, Worcester was incorporated in 1684. It was established as a township on June 14, 1722, chosen as the county seat of Worcester County in 1731, and incorporated as a city on February 29, 1848. With over 1,200 acres and a population of approximately 175,898, Worcester is the third largest city in New England.

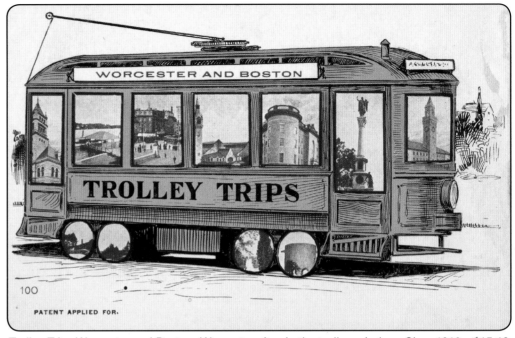

Trolley Trips Worcester and Boston. Worcester sites in the trolley window. *Circa 1910s, $15-18*

Greetings from Worcester, Mass. The city that is situated in the center of this rural grandeur, with beautiful Lake Quinsigamond at its eastern doors, the stately Asnebumskit on its western borders and the majestic Wachusett on the north. Published by J. I. Williams, Worcester, Mass. *Circa 1920s, $4-6*

Black and White Greetings from Worcester embellished with glitter. Cancelled. *Circa 1920s, $4-6*

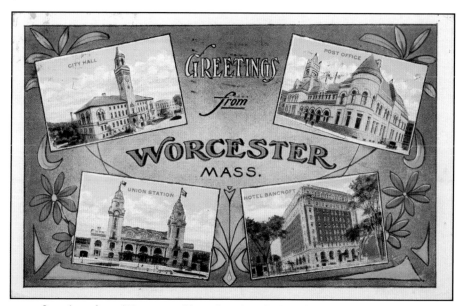

Greetings from Worcester, Mass. Imprinted with "Quality Service" surrounded a capital "W" for Worcester. *Cancelled Aug 14, 1925, $4-6*

Greetings from Worcester, Mass "The Heart of America." Printed at the Ideal Paper Supply Company, Worcester, MA. A genuine Curteich-Chicago "C.T. Art-Colortone" post card. *Circa 1940s, $3-4*

Like Rome, Worcester was built on seven hills: Pakachoag, Sagatabscot, Hancock, Chandler, Green, Bancroft, and Newton. It is situated in the center of rural grandeur, with beautiful Lake Quinsigamond to the east, stately Asnebumskit Mountain to the west, and majestic Wachusett Mountain to the north. Nature has endowed the region with beauty, and in the late 19th to mid-20th centuries her residents began a park system that was considered the pride of Worcester. Today it has 1,215 acres of public parklands and has evolved into an education, medical, and research center, with thirteen colleges and universities and five hospitals.

Worcester also proudly offers professional sports for every fan. Its professional football team, the New England Surge, and professional hockey team, the Worcester Sharks (of the American Hockey League) play their home games at the world-class auditorium, the DCU (Digital Credit Union) Center (formally known as the Centrum) in the heart of downtown Worcester. In addition, the Worcester Tornadoes, a professional independent minor league baseball team, plays home games at Hanover Park, on the campus of the College of the Holy Cross. This trifecta of baseball, hockey, and arena football means there is live sport for every season!

Worcester found its way into the history books with her multiples of "firsts." A good place to begin is Eli Whitney, who invented the cotton gin

The twenty-first-century skyline of Worcester, Massachusetts.

here. At Worcester, Elias Howe made the first sewing machine, the textile loom, and the corset, the all-night-lunch, envelopes, Valentines and post cards, the first women's college and the first public park were founded here. The first Bible, the first dictionary, and the largest newspaper of the time (the Massachusetts Spy) were printed in Worcester in the 18th century by Isaiah Thomas. In 1847 the first commercial valentine was mass produced in Worcester by Ester Howland. Worcester was host to the first national Women's Rights Convention in 1850 that Susan B. Anthony attended. The first steam calliope used especially on riverboats was patented by Joshua Stoddard in 1855. In a state known for its exceptional writers, the first ballpoint pen and the first typewriter were invented in Worcester, Massachusetts. Frances Perkins of Worcester was the first woman to serve on a president's cabinet serving as Franklin Delano Roosevelt's Secretary of Labor. Worcester launched the first liquid fuel rocket by "the father of modern rocketry," Robert Goddard, a graduate of Worcester Polytechnic Institute (WPI) and teacher at Clark University.

Worcester is also the home of Ted Williams' first home run at an exhibition game against Holy Cross College at Fitton Field in 1939 and to Bob Cousy, former basketball player for the Boston Celtics and a member of the Basketball Hall of Fame.

Dick the Derby Smith was first to introduce the Beatles to our country on Worcester's radio station WORC. Smith was given a Beatle's gold record with the inscription, To America's First Believer.

And of course, an icon that makes us all smile: the first Smiley Face. Worcester native and graphic artist Harvey Ball, was asked to create a design for the American Group Insurance Company's employees. He came up with the idea for a simple round yellow face with a huge smile and that was the beginning of our nation's love with the Smiley Face.

Many other Worcester residents made their marks on history. Two major anti-slavery leaders were also Worcester residents: Abby Kelley Foster and her husband Stephen Foster. Abby Kelley Foster's interests also extended to the rights of women. At the annual meeting of the American Anti-Slavery Society in 1840 when asked to withdraw her nomination to the business committee because she was a woman, she replied: "I rise to speak because I am not a slave."

Other residents of interest: John Adams, signer of the Declaration of Independence and the second President of the United States of America who taught school in Worcester; Albert A. Michelson, 1907 Nobel Prize Winner in Physics and a physics professor at Clark

University; Abbot Howard "Abbie" Hoffman, the famous radical of the 1960s, who coined the phrase "trust no one over 30"; Cole Porter, famous songwriter and graduate of Worcester Academy; Barbara Carole Coppersmith, aka Barbara Carroll, New York City jazz pianist; Bill Guerin, hockey player, Olympian and New Jersey Devils; Ron Darling, player for the New York Mets and Oakland; Jack Barry of the Boston Red Sox; Rich Gedman, Boston Red Sox all-star catcher; Tim Lahey, Phillies Pitcher; Major Taylor, cyclist who set the world speed record; Stanley Kunitz, Pulitzer Bollingen and National Medal of Arts winner; Nicholas Gage producer of The Godfather; journalist Rick Eid, writer and producer of Law and Order; Tony Randall, actor (who at one time worked for WTAG radio); George Kennedy and numerous other actors.

Worcester also has a conveniently located Regional Airport owned by the City and operated by the Massachusetts Port Authority. Originally named Whittall Field after the honorable Matthew John Whittall Superintendent of Crompton Carpet Mills and founder of Whittall Carpet Mills. The official opening and dedication of the Worcester Airport took place on Saturday, October 8th, 1927 with the Honorable Michael J. O'Hara, Mayor of Worcester, chairing the event.

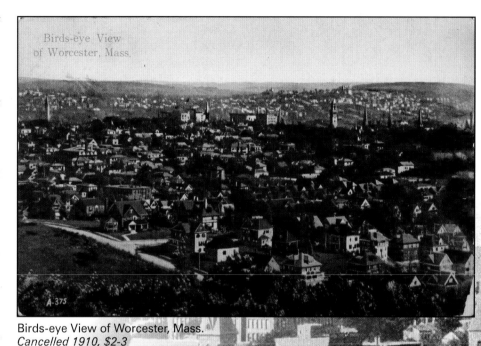

Birds-eye View of Worcester, Mass.
Cancelled 1910, $2-3

Bird's Eye View of Worcester, Mass, from State Mutual Building, looking south. *Cancelled 1908, $4-6*

8

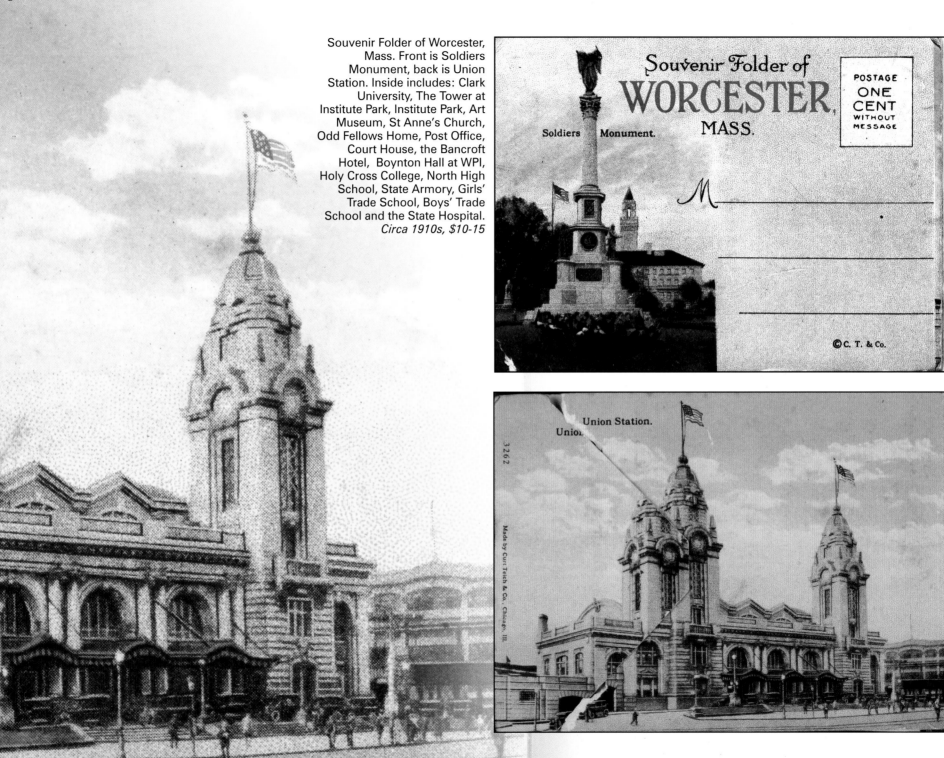

Souvenir Folder of Worcester, Mass. Front is Soldiers Monument, back is Union Station. Inside includes: Clark University, The Tower at Institute Park, Institute Park, Art Museum, St Anne's Church, Odd Fellows Home, Post Office, Court House, the Bancroft Hotel, Boynton Hall at WPI, Holy Cross College, North High School, State Armory, Girls' Trade School, Boys' Trade School and the State Hospital.
Circa 1910s, $10-15

Worcester Municipal Airport. *Cancelled 13 July 1961. $2-3*

Cover of Souvenir Program of the Worcester Air Pageant, Saturday Oct 8, 1927 dedication of the new Whittall Field, Worcester, Airport. *$25-30*

Today, Worcester Regional Airport offers a $15.7 million passenger terminal, which provides state-of-the-art passenger comfort and accessibility and features four jet way gates, two ramp level gates, two baggage carousels and a TSA installed passenger and baggage screening system. Currently, Worcester Regional Airport has no regularly scheduled commercial service and only has public Charter related activity. But all general aviation activity and services remain available. Last year Worcester Regional Airport had approximately 60,000 operations involving private, corporate commercial charter, military and general aviation.

Worcester with all of its history and modern contributions to Massachusetts and to our United States has developed into a world class city, in a desired location, with an affordable standard of living.

Chapter 2
Industry

Birthplace of the American Industrial Revolution

Situated along the Blackstone River Valley, which is known as the "birthplace of the American Industrial Revolution," Worcester is well known for her industrial innovations. In 1796, the Blackstone Canal was an idea of Providence, Rhode Island, businessman John Brown, who sought to open Rhode Island's coastal trade with Worcester. It was not until 1822 that the Canal was approved, and in 1823 the Blackstone Canal Company was incorporated. Thanks to engineer Benjamin Wright, the Blackstone Canal was opened in 1828 connecting Worcester to the world.

Credit is given to Stephen Salisbury II for the major influence he had in shaping Worcester's early industry. His father was one of the wealthiest men in Worcester and had acquired land around the Lincoln Square area. Upon his death his son inherited everything and turned land that was once used for farming into factories and tenements. It was through his efforts that Ichabod Washburn came to Worcester in 1818 and in 1831 established a company for making wire: Washburn and Moen. It was in 1876 when Joseph Glidden, the DeKalb, Illinois designer and patent holder for barb wire, sold his interest to his patent to Washburn and Moen which insured that Worcester became the largest maker of barbed wire in the country.

By the late 1800s Worcester rivaled New York and Philadelphia in the diversity of products manufactured; and the wire-producing Washburn and Moen factory, employing more than 2,000 people, was the largest and most important industry in Worcester. Fifty-eight percent of all the wire made in the United States (including barbed wire, piano wire, and wire for ladies corsets) was produced by Washburn & Moen Company. Washburn & Moen later became part of American Steel and Wire Company.

In 1864 David Hale Fanning established the Worcester Skirt Company where hoopskirts were manufactured. (Interestingly, Fanning also opened a girls trade school specializing in nursing, that became part of the Worcester Public School system in 1998, closed, then reopened in 2006 as the Worcester Technical High School.) By the 1900s Fanning's factory was producing corsets and the factory name was changed to the Royal Worcester Corset Company. It employed approximately 2,000 workers with 95 percent of the employees being women.

Historic view from the Bancroft Tower showing Institute Park, Worcester, Mass. *Cancelled 24 Jul 1911, $5-6*

American Steel and Wire Co., North Works, Worcester, MA. In script "April 2 - 1907 Bernard." *Cancelled Apr 2, 1907, $4-6*

American Steel & Wire Co., Dam, South Works, Worcester, Mass. *Cancelled July 17, 1907, $4-6*

Twenty-first-century photo of Washburn and Moen Manufacturing Company building. Today, the building houses restaurants, retail stores, a hair salon, and offices.

90 Grove Street Building, previously the home of Washburn and Moen Manufacturing Company.

Industrial Museum of the Worcester Pressed Steel Company. John Woodman founded the company and established the Higgins Armory Museum in order to give employees an idea of what types of things were created out of steel, and to appease his wife who one day found a suit of armor in her tub! *Circa 1910s, $6-8*

INDUSTRIAL MUSEUM OF THE WORCESTER PRESSED STEEL COMPANY
WORCESTER, MASS.

EMPLOYEES NOON-DAY LAWN PARTY
FACTORY of ROYAL WORCESTER CORSET CO
WORCESTER MASS

Employees Noon-Day Lawn Party, Factory of Royal Worcester Corset Co., Worcester, Mass. *Circa 1900s, $15-20*

CRIMPTON & KNOWLES LOOM WORKS
PHILADELPHIA, PA.   WORCESTER, MASSACHUSETTS   PROVIDENCE, R.I.

Compton & Knowles Loom Works, Worcester, Massachusetts, Looms for every type of textile fabric are manufactured here. Located on Grand Street, at the corner of Taintor Street. Card Published by J.I. Williams, Worcester, Mass, *Circa 1910s, $3-5*

An industry of loom-making was also developing. New loom-producing companies were attracted to Worcester because of two factors: the many skilled workers who could make the intricate parts of the loom mechanisms, and the existing near-by foundries that could make the larger parts of the looms. Compton & Knowles Loom Works was formed in 1897 when two competitors (George Crompton and Lucius Knowles) merged. Compton & Knowles became the largest and most successful plant that dominated the market for fancy looms in America and for woolen looms in the world - right through the mid 20th century.

Compton & Knowles Loom Works, Worcester, Massachusetts, *Circa 1910s, $4-5*

The brick factory building was home to Compton & Knowles Loom Works. Today, some of the building has been renovated for condominiums. Notice the close proximity to the railroad still in operation today.

Norton Emery and Wheel Company was established in the 1880s with beginnings in a pottery shop owned by Franklin B. Norton. Norton worked with a skilled potter named John Jeppson, an immigrant from Sweden to Worcester who founded Norton Emery and Wheel Company. This famous operation at One New Bond Street is the world's largest manufacturer and supplier for products including abrasives, grinding wheels, grinding and lapping machines, shapers and gear cutting machines, refractories and electro-chemicals. Norton Company held a prominent position in metal finishing and removal for more than a century. The "new bond" in the address came from development of the first vitrified wheel by employee, Swen Pulson. Norton began manufacturing synthetic grain in the late 1800s and opened a plant in Niagara Falls in 1901, events that brought about the name Norton Co. in 1906. Currently known as Saint-Gobain Abrasives Inc., the company occupies 156 acres and extends over two miles.

The Norton name is also associated with machine tools, with many of the old Norton machines still in use throughout industry today. Charles H. Norton (no relation) was a tireless advocate for grinding as a machining process. Norton Grinding Company joined forces with Norton Company in 1919; the company operated independently but had a common checkbook. This union plus the countless research reports, articles and books helped propel grinding into today's technology. Saint-Gobain acquired Norton Co. in 1990, but continues the Norton legacy producing its line of performance engineered abrasives for technical manufacturing and commercial applications as well as general household and automotive refinishing.

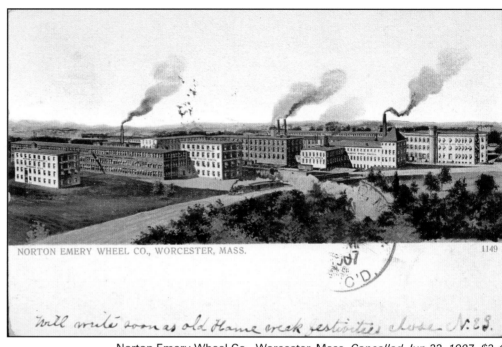

Norton Emery Wheel Co., Worcester, Mass. *Cancelled Jun 22, 1907, $3-4*

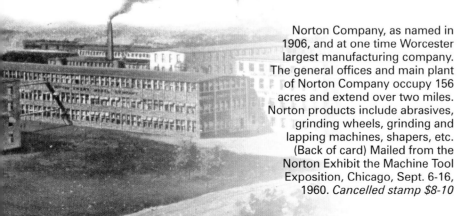

Norton Company, as named in 1906, and at one time Worcester largest manufacturing company. The general offices and main plant of Norton Company occupy 156 acres and extend over two miles. Norton products include abrasives, grinding wheels, grinding and lapping machines, shapers, etc. (Back of card) Mailed from the Norton Exhibit the Machine Tool Exposition, Chicago, Sept. 6-16, 1960. *Cancelled stamp $8-10*

Bradley Car Works was founded by Osgood Bradley in 1820 or 1822, and manufactured stage coaches, carriages, wagons, gigs and sleighs. In 1826, Bradley's company built coaches for the large stage line operators in New York and New England. Bradley was born in Andover, Massachusetts, but came to Worcester in 1820 where he opened a two-story shop. He later sold his company, but in 1833, again in business, he built the swell-sided bodies for road coaches. In 1835 Bradley built what is believed to be the first passenger train cars (railway coaches) built in the United States.

Even when his factory was at its full production Bradley's company was considered a poor financial risk. But he came up with a partner and the company was renamed Bradley and Rice. His cars were very popular and for a two year period were advertised in the prestigious American Railway Times.

Later, during the Civil War, Bradley's company produced gun carriages for the Union Army. His three sons John, Henry and Bradley Jr. came into the company and it was called Osgood Bradley and Sons for the next 19 years. In 1901, Osgood's grandson became president of the company. And by 1910, only the Pullman Works in Chicago was larger than the Osgood Bradley Company.

During this time, Standard Steel Car Company bought the Bradley Company and later Standard Steel merged with Pullman. In 1930 at the time of the sale and merger, the Osgood Bradley building was the only facet of Pullman that could fully assemble street car and trolley coaches. It closed in 1960. A coach baggage car, built in 1864 by Bradley for the Grand Trunk Railway is currently located at the Wisconsin Mid-Continent Railway Museum waiting for restoration.

In 1825, the Old Pine Meadow road was the main road from the east side of Worcester to the old common. Parley Goddard had a sandpit near that road - where the Worcester Brewing Company later was built. The pit was the chief supply of sand for the city of Worcester. William Eaton made bricks near the sand pit. The road began to cave in near the brick yard because of the sand pit, so the city officials told them that they had to quit working it. The remaining brick was used to pave the road. Years later, Mrs. Ella Hennesey bought the old deserted brickyard and old road. She sold it to White, Pevey and Dexter Company, who later sold the land to the Meat Trust. The old road and the brickyard lot seemed of no value, said Mrs. Boland, whose father once owned it.

Bradley Car Works, Worcester, Mass.

Bradley Car Works, Worcester, Mass. Located on West Mountain Street, formerly located at Washington Square but it had to move in 1909 to make way for the new Union Station. Published by the Rawson Post Card Co., Worcester, Mass. $10-15

White Pevey and Dexter Co., Worcester, Mass. The factory packed pork. *Cancelled Dec 16, 1911, $8-10*

Ester Howland is credited as being the first to mass produce Valentines in Worcester. Although, there is discussion that a Mr. Jotham Taft may have also been mass producing valentines in the nearby town of Grafton. It is certain that in 1879, Jotham Taft's son Edward and Ester Howland established the New England Valentine Company.

In 1863 George C. Whitney joined his brother Edward in the family stationery store and established Whitney Valentine Company of Worcester. In 1869 Edward resigned from the company. In 1881 George purchased the New England Valentine Company from Jotham Taft. Now, as sole owner, George incorporated the New England Valentine Company into Whitney Valentine Company.

Originally founded as a stationary store the Whitney Valentine Company became an important publisher and printer of Valentine's and other holiday cards along with postcards. Famous for Valentine's Day cards, George C. Whitney installed embossing and paper lace making machinery in his factory so he could manufacture every detail of the cards' components in his U.S. factory. His company produced post cards for every holiday - among the famous are the Nimble Nicks characters featured on his Christmas post cards. Production continued after George's death in 1915 when his son Warren took over the business. Whitney Valentine Company manufactured mechanical and holiday cards until the company closed its doors in 1942. Whitney cards can be identified by a red W or by the statement "Whitney Made Worcester Mass."

"All my days will be sunny if you'll be my Valentine" Whitney Made, Worcester, Mass Card *Circa 1910s, $3-4*

Valentine's Day Card, Whitney Made, Worcester, Mass. *Circa 1920s, $2-3*

18

"Whoo-oo-o's a fraid of ghosts?" Halloween-Greeting Whitney Made, Worcester, Mass Card *Circa 1910s, $25-30*

Halloween Greetings Whitney Made, Worcester, Mass Card Circa 1910s, $25-30

"A Happy Halloween" "May your spirits rise tonight, BY CAT! And follow the flight of the witch's bats May you tremble, shiver and quake with fright If you're superstitious on Halloween night" Whitney Made, Worcester, Mass Card *Circa 1910s, $25-30*

"May the witches brew, Good luck for you" Whitney Made, Worcester, Mass Card the largest manufacturer of valentines in the world it also manufactured postcards, art goods and novelties. *Circa 1910s, $25-30*

Thanksgiving Day Greetings Whitney Made, Worcester, Mass Card *Hand Cancelled with two cent stamp on 11-21-1921, $5-6*

THANKSGIVING DAY GREETINGS

I welcome this good season of mellow fruitfulness As just one more occasion to wish you happiness

Here's hoping you'll have a very happy Thanksgiving Day

"Here's hoping you'll have a very happy Thanksgiving Day" Whitney Made, Worcester, Mass Card *Circa 1910s, $5-6*

"By this little card you'll see how nimble Nimble Nicks can be." Whitney Made, Worcester, Mass Card *Circa 1910s, $15-20*

"These gay Nimble Nicks have come to say I wish you loads of fun on Christmas Day" Whitney Made, Worcester, Mass Die Cut Card, *Circa 1910, $20-$25*

"All through the year kind wishes I've safely stored away, For Santa Claus to bring to you on Christmas Day" Whitney Made, Worcester, Mass Card, *Cancelled Dec 23, 1905, $15-20*

Uncle Sam has brought us a long, long way
To wish you a jolly, and a Merry Christmas day,
He jolted us and banged us and shook us all about
For everybody's busy all along the route.

"Uncle Sam has brought us a long long way to wish you a jolly, and a Merry Christmas day. He jolted us and banged us and shook us all about for everybody's busy all along the route." Whitney Made, Worcester, Mass Card *Dated 1917, $6-8*

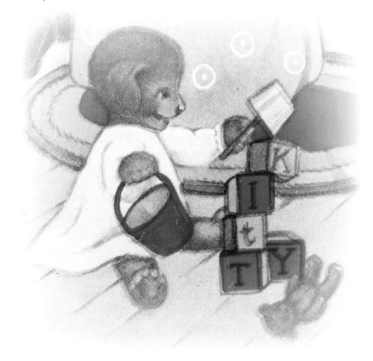

"Merry Christmas" Whitney Made, Worcester, Mass Card with dogs, *Circa 1910s, $15-20*

From over the hills and far away
This card comes speeding to you to say
I WISH YOU A MERRY CHRISTMAS

"From over the hills and far away this card comes speeding to you to say I WISH YOU A MERRY CHRISTMAS" Whitney Made, Worcester, Mass Card two cancelled one cent stamps illegible date, *Circa 1910s, $3-4*

I signad juletid

Det löfte jag
ej glömma vill,
att himmelriket
dem hör till,
som hafua barnasinne

Christmas Card in German, Whitney Made, Worcester, Mass Card, *Circa 1910s, $4-5*

New Year Card with winter, spring, summer, autumn "May the little new Year and his friends so gay, Leave with you their blessings, ere they haste away, Whitney Made, Worcester, Mass Card *Circa 1910s, $10-15*

New Year Greeting Card, Whitney Made, Worcester, Mass Card *Circa 1910s, Cancelled Dec 31, Dedham Heights, Mass, $3-4*

"These ducks just from meeting Bring you my Easter Greeting" Whitney Made, Worcester, Mass Card *Circa 1910s, $5-6*

"Chick-A-Biddy and I wish you a glad Easter"
Cancelled Apr 11, 1908, Whitney Made, Worcester, Mass Card, $5-6

Easter Greeting Card, Whitney
Made, Worcester, Mass Card
Dated Apr 20, 1924, $3-4

EASTER GREETING

Easter Greeting Card, Whitney Made, Worcester, Mass Card
Circa 1920s, $3-4

Easter Greeting Card "Alleluia" Whitney Made, Worcester, Mass Card
Dated Apr 20, 1924, $3-4

Happy Easter Card, Whitney
Made, Worcester, Mass Card
Circa 1910s, $3-4

HAPPY EASTER

Every blossom on the tree
Every little bird outside
All combine to wish with me
For you a Happy Eastertide

EASTER GREETINGS

Easter Time is a friendly
time,
And just the time to say.
I wish that joy may bloom anew,
Like flowers on Easter Day.

Easter Greeting Card, Whitney Made, Worcester, Mass Card *Cancelled Mar 27, illegible year, Circa 1910s, $3-4*

Birthday Greeting "A Happy Birthday" Whitney Made, Worcester, Mass Card, *Circa 1910s, $3-4*

I HOPE YOU'LL HAVE
A HAPPY BIRTHDAY

Birthday Greeting "I Hope You'll Have A Happy Birthday" Whitney Made, Worcester, Mass Card, *Circa 1910s, $3-4*

The prominent Samuel Porter family owned and operated the Samuel Porter (Shoe) Last Manufacturing Company on Union Street in Worcester. They made the wooden molds that shoes were built around. In 1865, the Porter's had a son they named Walter. By the 1900s Walter was the companies representative and he and two other businessmen (G. Clifford, the president of Belcher Last Co. in Stoughton MA, and J. Maguire of Dunbar Pattern Co. in Brockton MA) traveled abroad to further increase foreign business. Unfortunately, their return trip to America was booked first class on the Titanic and all three perished. Clifford and Maguire were never found; Porter's body was discovered by the rescue ship MacKay Bennett.

In 1941, Worcester's David Clark designed, developed and manufactured air and space equipment, including the first space suits worn in 1965 during the first space walks by Ed White, Chuck Yeager, and Neil Armstrong. David Clark Company Inc. made the space suits worn by NASA Gemini and Apollo astronauts and developed the first anti-G suit, so speed does not affect jet pilots of today. The company continues to excel in the production of aerospace products including suits worn by modern space shuttle astronauts.

There are a number of other businesses that had their beginnings in the late 1700s and early 1800s that are currently flourishing in Worcester. They include the following. The Marble-Nye Company established in 1770. Interestingly, Mr. and Mrs. Arthur E. Nye were in Europe on business for J. Russell Marble. Because of the coal strike, there was a delay in some of the business meetings. Rather than miss the meetings, Mr. Nye canceled his reservations on the Titanic Maiden Voyage. They came home a few days later on the George Washington, sailing on the same route as the Titanic passing a number of icebergs as they sailed. When Mr. Nye returned to work at the bakery, he was congratulated by his friends that he had such good luck as not to have been on the Titanic.

The Elwood Adams Hardware Store (1782) carries the title of the oldest hardware store in the USA. The first owner Daniel Waldo sold, bought and traded saddles, oil lamps, and hand tools. It changed hands a number of times: in the 1820s Henry Miller bought the store; in 1869, a young apprentice - Elwood Adams - bought it and changed the name; and in 1958 two Frenchmen Cloutier and Champagne bought the store. The Cloutier family still runs the hardware store. Paul, James and sister Marie with their experienced staff specialize in hard-to-find items.

The Putnam family was prominent in Worcester for many years as attorneys, town officials and a bank president. They were affiliated with Barnard, Sumner & Putnam Co (1819). When the Merchants & Farmers Mutual Insurance Co. was first incorporated (1846), Isaac Davis was president and Charles Putnam was secretary.

In 1826, the Heald Machine Company made grinding machine tools in Worcester employing 1300 workers and owning a complex of 35 acres in Greendale area, with nearly 500,000 square feet of buildings. In 1992, it closed its doors. Edward C. Camp bought most of the inventory and continues to successfully manufacture grinding machines.

Royal Worcester Trade Card for the Worlds Columbian Exposition, Chicago, 1893. $20-25

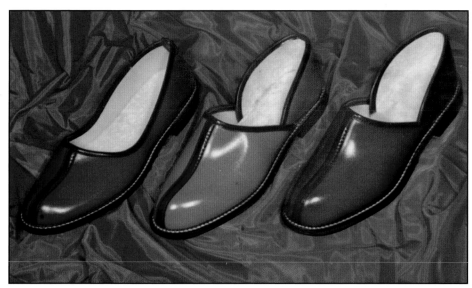

Pan-American Shoe Mfg Co., Inc., located at 65 Beacon Street, Worcester, MA sold men's shearling slippers. *$3-4*

Located in Worcester, Massachusetts, this modern handsome building amidst beautifully landscaped grounds is headquarters of the America Group and home office for four of the companies: State Mutual Life Assurance Co., of America, Worcester Mutual Fire Insurance Com., Guarantee Mutual Assurance Co., of America and American Variable Annuity Life Assurance Company. (As written on the back) *$3-4*

Trade Card from Samuel Winslow, Manufacturer of Ice and Roller Skates, Worcester, Mass. *Circa 1900, $10-12*

Rural Cemetery, Inc. (1838) is now called Rural Cemetery and Crematory and is located on Grove Street. J.S. Wesby & Sons (1847) is still located on Portland Street. The Ross Brothers Co (1843) still sells red paint. While in business in 1942, State Mutual Life Assurance Co (1844), sent letters to potential clients - explaining how Americans heading home from Europe "could live through the same day twice" as they traveled over the International Date Line. The letter (which included a map of the date line) went on to state that "Here in this country we can not live a day over again." The company was encouraging their clients to buy life insurance. It must have worked as they are still in business today. Washburn & Garfield Co. (1846) sells piping and tubing (industrial controls) and since 1872 has been located on the corner of Prescott Street.

Rural Cemetery and Crematory located on Grove Street.

In 2004/2005 a collaborative effort began in Worcester for the acquisition, renovation and reconstruction of industrial business buildings for lease in a 63 acre area. This project is known as Gateway Park named after Gateway Park LLC who along with WPI and the Worcester Business Development Corporation planned the development of this area. A grant of almost 3 million dollars was submitted to the United States Economic Development Administration. In 2008 the Life Sciences and Bioengineering Center, a redevelopment of a Worcester Brownfield, was built on eleven acres in the park.

The Northern Gateway Visitor Center was also developed in the historic Washburn-Moen Wireworks building. The 65,000-square-foot building contains tourist information, exhibits, shops, restaurant and offices.

Gateway Park, a Brownfield redevelopment project.

Gateway Park sign, a collaborative effort among engineers, the city, and the WPI.

The completed WPI Life Science Bioengineering facility and parking garage.

Gateway Park sign.

Chapter 3
Downtown

Renovation is nothing new to the city of Worcester. In 1897 a Romanesque Revival-style Post Office was built on Franklin Square. In 1930, a new Worcester Post Office and Courthouse designed by James Wetmore was built on that site, at the southern end of the Worcester business district on Lincoln Square. Along with the new courthouse, Worcester War Memorial Auditorium and an extension of the Worcester Art Museum were also built in 1930.

Rare leather postcard of City Hall, Worcester, Mass. *Cancelled Sep 25, 1906, $10-15*

City Hall Plaza, Worcester, Mass showing flower beds protected by Wheelock Fence Guard made by Wright Wire Company, Worcester, Mass. *Circa 1910, $4-5*

City Hall, Worcester, Mass.

City Hall, Worcester, Mass. *Cancelled Dec 17, 1910, $3-4*

CITY HALL, WORCESTER, MASS.   4A-H260

View of City Hall on a Genuine Curteich-Chicago "C.T. Art-Colortone" Linen Post Card from Ideal Paper Supply Co., Worcester, Mass. Ca., *1920s, $5-6*

City Hall Plaza, Park Building and Post Office in the distance. Pub.by Perkins & Butler, Inc., Worcester, Mass., Ca., *1920s, $5-6*

Rear View of City Hall and Park, *Cancelled Aug 20, 1914, $3-4*

Soldiers' monument, City Hall and Common, Pub.by Perkins & Butler, Inc., Worcester, Mass., Ca., *1920s, $5-6*

SOLDIERS' MONUMENT & COMMON, WORCESTER, MASS.

The Soldiers' Monument & Common splendidly laid out with many shady trees and settees. The Hotel Bancroft, City Hall and busiest section of Worcester are situated around the Common. *Cancelled Jun 28, $3-4*

721. SOLDIERS' MONUMENT, WORCESTER, MASS.

Soldiers' Monument, Worcester, Mass., sculpted by Randolph Rogers. The inscription reads: "Erected by the people of Worcester to the memory of her sons who died for the unity of the republic. A.D. 1861-1865." The monument was dedicated on July 15, 1874. Card for the Metropolitan News Co., Boston, *Cancelled Dec 1, 1906, $2-3*

Timothy Bigelow Monument located on the Common was erected in honor of the Revolutionary War patriot, Colonel Timothy Bigelow. The monument was dedicated on April 19, 1861. *Cancelled Dec 4, 1911, $2-3*

A Bronze Statue of Senator George Frisbie Hoar, a Harvard grad and Worcester lawyer who was elected and served in the United States Senate from 1877-1904. The statue was dedicated in 1908. *Cancelled Circa 1910, $3-4*

40

In the 1970s, a third new Post Office was built in Worcester - on Summer Street - and the 1930s Post Office and Courthouse had major interior renovation. It was renamed the Harold Donohue Federal Building and Courthouse honoring Harold Donohue a US Representative.

The first Worcester Post Office was established in 1775 with Isaiah Thomas as postmaster. In 1897 the new government building was opened at the cost of $400,000. At the time it was one of the best in the country. Published by J.I. Williams, Worcester, MA. *Circa 1900, $5-6*

This Worcester Post Office was constructed in 1930-1931 as a post office, courthouse and federal building. A "Colourpicture" Card published by Economy Distributors, Inc., Worcester, Mass. *Circa 1930s, $4-5*

Another view of the handsome Worcester Post Office in 1897.
Circa 1900, $3-4

Nearly 80 years later, in the fall of 2007, Worcester again saw renovation. A new 180-million-dollar downtown Worcester court house (named Worcester Trial Courthouse) opened its doors. The celebration was attended by Massachusetts governor, Deval Patrick, the Lt Governor (and Worcester native) Tim Murray, state senators, Chief Justices, judges, lawyers and many interested citizens of Worcester. Governor Patrick stated: "Throughout history, Massachusetts has advanced America's pursuit of equality, opportunity and fair play to every citizen. Today we welcome this court to that legacy. Thanks to the hard work and commitment of our state and local officials and all members of the community, this courthouse 'the largest in the Commonwealth' has become a reality." Chief Justice Mulligan stated: "Today we make history as the halls of justice in Worcester move into the 21st century. The beauty, functionality and solidity displayed here underscore our commitment that all who come to this courthouse will understand justice as the essential cornerstone of a free society."

The Worcester County Court House and Statue of General Charles Devens, a noted Civil War officer, jurist and statesman, was erected on Court Hill in 1736. This building was completed in 1900. Card pub by Perkins & Butler, Inc., Worcester, *Circa 1920s, $3-4*

The Worcester Court House with the American Antiquarian Society's second headquarters on the right - it was torn down in 1910 - in order to allow for the Court House expansion. Over the entrance are chiseled the words: "OBEDIENCE TO LAW IS LIBERTY" *Cancelled Jul 10, 1908, $2-3*

General Charles Devens statue unveiled on July 4, 1906. Devens a distinguished veteran was commissioned a Major General and in 1877 appointed Attorney General of the United States of America by President Hayes. *Cancelled May 21, 1914, $3-4*

Designed by Shepley, Bulfinch, Richardson and Abbott Architects and built by Gilbane Building Company, the new Court House houses the District, Housing, Juvenile, Probate, Family and the Superior Courts. The building is handicap accessible, has four stories, twenty-six court rooms, many conference and jury deliberation rooms, detention areas and a café. In addition, there is plenty of public parking just a block away. The old courthouse may be renovated to be used as a museum, a law school or perhaps a hotel or residential building. The annex built on the back of the beautiful building would be torn down but the facade built in 1899 would be preserved.

New Court House, completed in 2008.

The first Union Station, Foster Street, *Circa 1875. Cancelled Apr 12, 1909, $7-8*

The National Park Service and U.S. Department of the Interior credit the Blackstone River Valley (the Canal being the catalyst) with the birthplace of the American Industrial Revolution. The services of the canal were short lived with the advent of the railroad in 1832. Railroads were coming into Worcester and by 1847 the Boston Passenger House (also called the Boston and Worcester Depot) was built on Foster and Norwich Street. As the primary rail depot by the 1870s it could no longer handle the increasing rail traffic. A station was designed by architects Ware and Van Brunt, and in 1874 to 1875 the construction of the first Union Passenger Station began. Opened on June 1, 1875 (on the site of Elliot Swan's Washington Square Hotel on the northwest corner of Washington Square) the clock tower instantly became the focal point of the city and the station was the Grand Central Station for all passing through Worcester.

Once again with the popularity of rail travel and the volume of more than ten thousand passengers daily, by 1898, the construction of a new Union Station was necessary. In 1901 the construction of the present Union Station began. Completed in 1911 with construction costs of $750,000 the building was nick-named the Million Dollar Union Station. Constructed using iron, cast iron and granite, along with state-of-the-art designed including twin towers, a clock and handsome canopies, Union Station had all of the modern conveniences of the era.

Sadly, with automobiles and air travel becoming more accessible to the public, by the 1920s rail travel began to decline. In 1926 due to safety concerns the twin towers were removed and in 1941 the canopies were removed. By 1959 Union Passenger Station was demolished and in 1964 the last passenger debarked the train from Union Station. Closed in 1972 the building was largely destroyed and became a white elephant near the heart of downtown Worcester. Union Station was bought and sold from 1983 until 1994 when the Worcester Redevelopment Authority bought the building. Currently magnificently restored, Union Station is an active train station once again!

Present Union Station in Washington Square, with original marble towers. Construction began in 1909 completed in 1911. Cost of the building was $750,000. Card Pub by J.I. Williams, Worcester, Mass. *Circa 1910, $6-7*

UNION STATION. WORCESTER. MASS.

Union Station after the twin towers were removed in 1926. Tichnor Quality Views Card, *Circa 1920s, $4-5*

Interior of Union Station, from here arrive and depart the trains of the Boston & Albany RR., N.Y., N.H., & H.R.R., Boston & Maine R.R., Norwich R.R. and Providence & Worcester R.R. Card pub by Henry Freeman & Co., Worcester, Mass. *Cancelled May 13, 1915, $7-8*

INTERIOR OF UNION STATION, WORCESTER, MASS.

MAIN STREET, FROM HARRINGTON CORNER, WORCESTER, MASS.

Today Worcester has many restaurants to please even the most picky connoisseur. The many cultures, diverse population and rich ethnic texture ensure there are restaurants of all kinds. It was Charles Palmer an inventor with innovative thinking who received the first patent in 1891 for his diner or lunch wagon. Mac's Diner (on Shrewsbury Street) is still owned and operated by members of the original owner's family and is a great place for delicious dining on a dime. And the Broadway, currently owned by the Feldman family, at 100 Water Street still serves their famous ice-cream.

Main Street from Harrington Corner. Notice the name of the building on second floor, it is cut into granite. *Circa, 1900s, $5-6*

Main Street and Harrington Corner, named after William Harrington who erected the four story building in the right corner, with City Hall here this was the hub of Worcester downtown. *Cancelled Nov 17, 1907, $3-4*

2583—Harrington Corner, Worcester, Mass.

Souvenir Post Card Co., New York and Berlin.

Worcester Mass., Main Street from Park Street. Notice the State Mutual building, the white building in the background, which is considered Worcester's first modern office building.
Cancelled Jul 29, 1911, $3-4

Worcester, Mass., Main Street from Park.

Main Street looking North from Park Street at night.
Cancelled Dec 1, 1916, $3-4

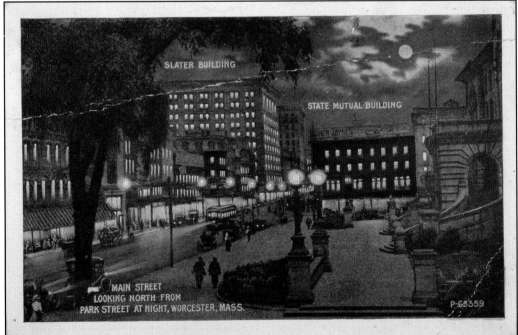

SLATER BUILDING

STATE MUTUAL BUILDING

MAIN STREET
LOOKING NORTH FROM
PARK STREET AT NIGHT, WORCESTER, MASS.

P-63359

Worcester Franklin Square, Junction of Main and South Bridge Streets. Notice the Telegram sign. The Telegram & Gazette known locally as the Telegram or the T&G established in 1884 as a Sunday paper, currently it is a subsidiary of The New York Times Company and since 1980 has been the only daily newspaper in Worcester. *Circa 1910s, $4-5*

Worcester Market, at the corner of Main and Madison Streets, opened in November 1914 as the newest and largest market so that the people of Worcester might have every facility for marketing. *Circa 1915, $10-15*

Denholm & McKay Co., Boston Store, Worcester, Mass. "Central Massachusett's largest Department Store, occupying nearly six acres of floor space. It is located at 484 to 500 Main Street - the heart of Worcester's busiest shopping district." *Stamped but not cancelled, Circa 1910s, $7-8*

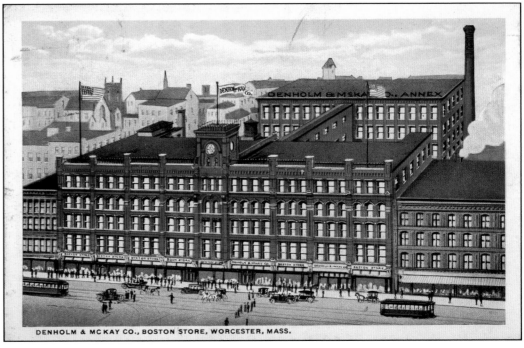

Worcester County Institution for Savings, South corner of Main and Foster Streets. The 11th Savings Bank chartered in the state, opened the doors on Oct 29, 1906. *Cancelled Sept 17, 1907, $4-5*

SLATER BUILDING, MAIN STREET, WORCESTER, MASS.

Slater Building, 390 Main Street, built in 1907, designed by Frosts, Briggs and Chamberlain, Colonial Revival built to honor Samuel Slater. This building was the city's "second highest building or skyscraper" in 1907. *Cancelled Aug 23, 1904, $3-4*

State Mutual Building, Worcester, Mass.

BOOK BINDERS

State Mutual Building, 240 Main Street, built in 1870 is an example of Second Empire style. The first headquarters for State Mutual Life Assurance Company (now Allmerica Financial). *Cancelled Jun 10, 1910, $3-4*

TELEPHONE BUILDING, WORCESTER, MASS.

63324

Telephone Building. *Cancelled Jun 20, 1917 with Industry-Agriculture for Defense Postage Stamp, $4-5*

52

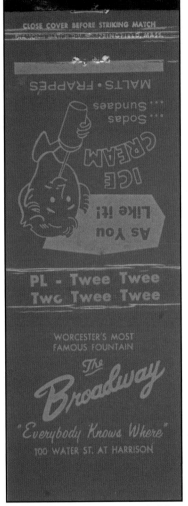

The Broadway "Worcester's Most Famous Fountain - Everybody Knows Where - 100 Water Street at Harrison" A family favorite currently owned by the Feldman Family. Match Book Cover
Circa 1950s, $2-3

Putnam & Thurston's Restaurant, 19-27 Mechanic Street, Worcester, Established in 1858 and it was "Worcester's Largest Restaurant with the Hunting and Spanish Rooms for breakfast, lunch and dinner, Dining and Dancing with Professional Floor Shows Every Night, Six Banquet Rooms for Parties of 4 to 500,"
$3-4

1929 F.W. Woolworth Store, 40 Front Street, Worcester, previously the Besse Bryant & Co., established ca. 1893 went out of business in 1928. Card
Circa 1940s, $4-5

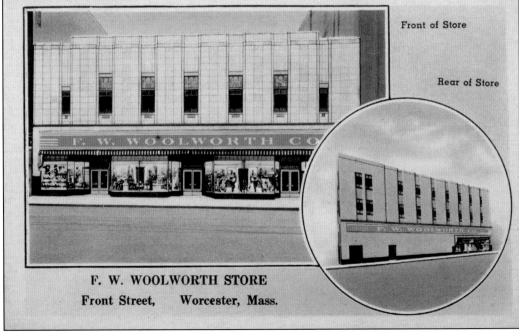

Wreck of Kane's Furniture Store, Worcester, Mass. The Great New England Hurricane of 1938. "September 21, 1938, will long be remembered as the date of the Big Hurricane which swept New England - in all history something never before known to this part of the country. The loss of lives was appalling' property damage mounted to hundreds of millions of dollars and the homeless counted to hundreds of thousands. The tremendous fury of the wind left behind destruction, destitution and utter ruin." *Circa 1940s, $8-9*

Wreck of Kane's Furniture Store. Worcester, Mass.

THE GREAT NEW ENGLAND HURRICANE OF 1938

Central Fire Station, 79 Foster Street was built in 1899 and demolished in 1955. The first brass sliding pole used in the country was in the city of Worcester in 1880. And although many things have changed in the city one thing remains constant "the Worcester Fire Department and its Firefighters, both past and present, are dedicated to: THE PROTECTION OF THE LIVES AND PROPERTY OF THE CITIZENS OF WORCESTER." Card *Circa 1910, $3-4*

Worcester, Mass., Central Fire Station.

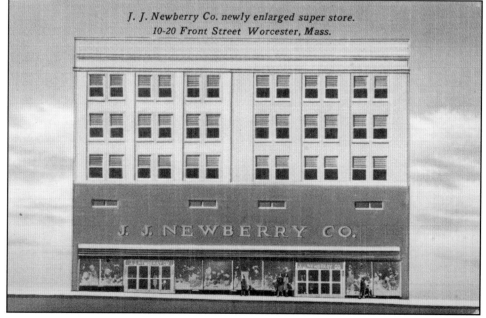

J.J. Newberry Co. newly enlarged super store. 10-20 Front Street. Worcester, Mass. *Circa 1940s, $5-6*

Elm Street View, on the left is the Worcester Club making its home in the former Isaac Davis mansion. Founded in 1888 as a men's social club until 1989 when women were allowed to become full members. Currently a private club with excellent cuisine and atmosphere. *Cancelled Feb 26, 1906. $2-3*

ELM ST. VIEW, WORCESTER, MASS.

Elm Street (looking toward Main St.). Notice on the right the columns of the Worcester Public Library. *Cancelled Nov 12, 1912, $2-3*

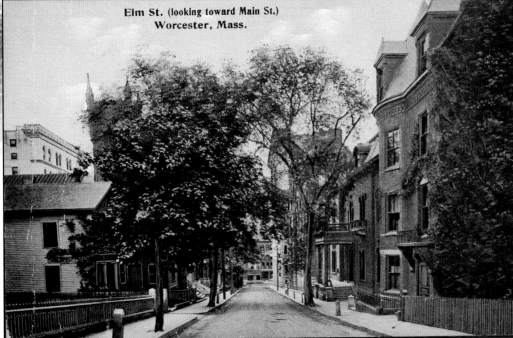

Elm St. (looking toward Main St.)
Worcester, Mass.

Worcester Public Library,
Elm Street.
Circa 1915, $3-4

PUBLIC LIBRARY, WORCESTER, MASS.

Public Library,
Worcester, Mass.

Worcester Public Library, Elm
Street. *Cancelled May 16, 1915,
$2-3*

Inside of the Worcester Public Library, Salem Square. *Circa 1950s, $2-3*

Worcester Public Library, Salem Square at Night, *Circa 1950s, $2-3*

57

The Bay State House, opened in 1856 as a first-class hotel. In
1942 it was reduced to two floors and is used as office buildings.
Cancelled Sep 10, 1909, $3-4

58

On Franklin Street, the Hotel Bancroft "Recognized as one of America's Finest Hotels" *Circa 1915, $4-5*

The Bancroft Hotel "Heaven" writes the author of this card. *Cancelled May 2, 1913, $4-5*

The Hotel Bancroft "This is supposed to be sweller than any hotel in N.Y. City." writes the author of this card. *Cancelled Nov 27, 1913, $4-5*

SHERATON-WORCESTER HOTEL
and Motor Inn, Worcester, Mass.

"The new Sheraton-Worcester Hotel and Motor Inn awaits you with a drive in welcome"…Free Reservations by Reservation - Reserves and confirms your Hotel Room in 4 seconds." *Card 1942-1955, $5-6*

In 1942 the Hotel Bancroft was sold to the Sheraton Hotel chain who renamed the Bancroft the Sheraton. The name reverted back to the Bancroft in 1955. In 1964 it was converted into apartments and retail. *Circa 1940s, $4-5*

60

The Holiday Inn. In 2004/5 this building was converted into upscale condominiums with close proximity to the downtown and Massachusetts College of Pharmacy and Health Sciences. Card *Circa 1940s, $2-3*

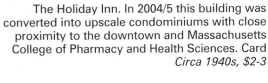

The Holiday Inn of Worcester "Delightful dining enjoyment awaits you at the Holiday Inn of Worcester in the Persian Room Restaurant. *Circa 1950s, $2-3*

The Hotel Standish was built in the late 1890s at Main and Jackson Streets. A "C.H. Prentice, Prop."
$4-5

HOTEL STANDISH

MAIN AND JACKSON STS., WORCESTER, MASS.

C. H. PRENTICE. PROP.

"THE WARREN", WORCESTER, MASS.

In 1892 through the mid twentieth century, The Warren Hotel stood at 199-207 Front Street.
Cancelled 17 Jul 1913, $2-3

Filene's at Worcester Center. "Facing the Common with its glistening pool, this center contains over 100 shops; department stores; restaurants and commercial buildings. This outstanding urban development, located in the core of Central new England, is backed by an indoor parking area for over 4,300 cars." Located in downtown, the Worcester Common Fashion Outlet Mall, originally opened as the Worcester Center Galleria on July 29, 1971. In 1996, its name was shortened simply to Worcester Common Outlets but by April 2006 the mall was closed, shutting for good. Currently there is exciting redevelopment taking place known as CitySquare. *Circa 1970s, $2-3*

Called the Centrum, Worcester Centrum, Worcester's Centrum Centre and as of 2004 the DCU (Digital Federal Credit Union) Center is a "multi-purpose civic center facility in Central Massachusetts is less than one hour from Boston, Springfield, Sturbride, Nashus, N.H., Providence, R.I. or Hartford, Ct." The facility hosts events to include: concerts, sporting events, family shows, conventions, trade shows and meetings. Owned by the City of Worcester it is managed by SMG a private management firm. *Circa 1970s, $2-3*

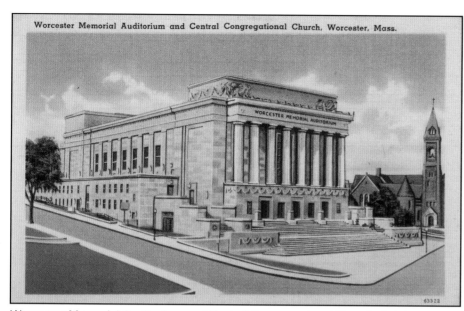

Worcester Memorial Auditorium and Central Congregational Church. Pub.by Perkins& Butler, Inc., Worcester, Mass. *Circa 1910s, $3-4*

"View showing Armory, Women's Club Building and North High School, Worcester, Mass." Pub. By Perkins & Butler, Inc., Worcester, Mass. *Circa 1940s, $4-5*

Worcester Memorial Auditorium and Worcester Boys' Club. *Printed 1964, $1-2*

Armory and Salisbury Street. Erected in 1889 dedicated on Jan 30, 1891. Notice the Salisbury Street School tower. *Cancelled Mar 1, 1912, $4-5*

64

The Woman's Club Building, Salisbury and Tuckerman Streets. Organized in 1880 this was the most exclusive organization for women in the city. *Cancelled Sep 22, 1907, $6-7*

"Dutch Suite, View 1, Woman's Club Building, Worcester, Mass. *Copyright, 1907 by T.C. Wohlbruck,"* $5-6

"Worcester Girls Club Camp - The Pool - Brushing Time - Nature Lore"
Cancelled Aug 1, 1942 on the back states "Buy Defense Bands and Stamps," $8-10

"Worcester Girls' Club" Pub by the Jones Supply Co., Worcester, Mass. *Circa 1910s, $8-10*

"This beautiful swimming pool is open to all people." Y.W.C.A. facility at 1 Salem Square built in the 1960's. Today the facility has a full fledged child care center with Daybreak Resources for Women and Children. *Card 1967, $1-2*

"Old Ladies' Home, 1183 Main Street, Worcester, Mass" Occupied on May 21, 1896. The Home for Aged Women founded by Ichabod Washburn, who left a large portion of his estate towards its endowment. *Cancelled 1905, $4-5*

Y.W.C.A. founded in 1885, took occupancy of this building in 1891/1892 with room for fifty women. A gym and facilities for education were added in 1915. In 1920 a new activities building with a swimming pool was built. Card *Circa, 1912, $4-5*

Boys Club, Worcester, MASS. *Circa 1920s $3-4*

"Odd Fellows Home, Worcester, Mass. At Greendale, this is an institution for both men and women, supported by the lodges of the order in Massachusetts, and is splendidly equipped." The home located at 104 Randolph Road was donated by patent attorney Thomas H. Dodge and it opened in 1892 to care for members of the order and their wives or widows. Card Pub. By Henry Freeman & Co., Worcester, Mass., *circa 1910s, $4-5*

"Odd Fellows Building, Main Street, Worcester, Mass." Located at 674 Main Street, dedicated on Nov 8, 1906 "…all for the use of the City's Odd Fellows" *Circa 1910s, $5-6*

Levana Club, Lincoln Square, Worcester, Mass. Hand-colored by T.C. Wohlbruck.
Cancelled 13 Feb 1911, $6-7

"Worcester Country Club, One of the Finest Tournament Courses in the East, Worcester, Mass. W-11" An exclusive members only club in Worcester. Card published by Economy Distributors, Inc., Worcester, Mass.
Cancelled Aug 29, 1946, $7-8

Twenty-first-century street view of
the old Court House.

Twenty-first-century front view of
the old Court House.

George Frisbie Hoar, seated on his bronze monument exactly where he was placed in 1908. Today, his spectacles are the only things missing from the original monument.

Twenty-first century Telegram and Gazette building, Franklin Street.

Twenty-first-century photograph of Tickerman Hall, Main Street.

Twenty-first-century photo of Dunkin' Donuts at Harrington Corner.

Still serving in the twenty-first century at Chadwick Square Diner off Grove Street.

Chapter 4
Attractions

Worcester residents have been at the forefront of innovation in the world of preservation whether it be art, armory, documents or parks; thus it is home to many museums. In 1812 Isaiah Thomas founded the Worcester Antiquarian Society. Originally located at the corner of Highland Street and Court House Hill it is now located at the corner of Park Avenue and Salisbury Street.

American Antiquarian Society. *Cancelled Sep 10, 1946, $3-4*

Twenty-first-century photo of Salisbury Mansion, built in 1772. It is owned and operated today by the Worcester Historical Museum.

American Antiquarian Society, Worcester Massachusetts. "A national library of historical references with over half a million titles relating to America." Organized in 1875 as the Worcester Society of Antiquity and originally located at the corner of Highland Street and Court House Hill. It changed to current name in 1919 and the building is currently located at Park Avenue and Salisbury Street. *Circa 1950s, $2-3*

Stephen Salisbury, an innovative thinker who among his many contributions to the city of Worcester, came up with the idea of the Worcester Art Museum. On February 25, 1896, at a meeting at his home with 50 other Worcester residents, Mr. Salisbury donated the acre of land on Salisbury Street for the building and $100,000 - half for the buildings construction and the rest going to an endowment fund. The Worcester Art Museum was designed by Stephen C. Earle a Worcester architect and opened its doors on May 10, 1898. Today it is one of the largest museums in New England.

Worcester Art Museum, *circa 1940s* published by Perkins & Butlre, Inc., Worcester, Mass. *$3-4*

The Worcester Art Museum opened on May 10, 1898. One of the largest in New England, designed by Worcester architect Stephen C. Earle built on land donated by Stephen Salisbury III. Back of the card states: "Rapheal Tuck & Sons Post Card Series No 1057, "Worcester, Mass." ART PUBLISHERS TO THEIR MAJESTIES THE KING AND QUEEN." *Circa 1910, $3-4*

Park Theatre, Front Street, Worcester, Mass., opened in 1857. (The assassin of President Lincoln, John Wilkes Booth, played there in 1863.) *Cancelled Mar 23, 1906, $8-10*

ARK THEATRE, WORCESTER, MASS.

POLI'S THEATRE, WORCESTER, MASS.

Poli's Theatre was owned by Sylvester Z. Poli who redesigned the Crompton Block on Mechanics Street after it was gutted by fire in 1905 with this ostentatious entry on 28 Front Street. The Theatre was used by companies, vaudeville houses and later motion pictures. *Circa 1910, $8-9*

WORCESTER THEATRE, WORCESTER, MASS.

The original Worcester Theatre, 20 Exchange Street, opened in 1869 and burned down in 1889. This is the new Worcester Theatre in 1897, razed in 1938. *Circa 1910, $8-10*

Mechanics Hall located at 321 Main Street is called *"the showpiece of a city where the arts thrive,"* by Horizon Magazine and has been judged by architectural historians and is noted as the nation's finest pre-Civil War concert hall. For nearly 150 years, Mechanics Hall (or the Hall) has been the cultural cornerstone of Central Massachusetts and is ideally located in downtown Worcester. It is listed in the National Register of Historic Places.

In 1842, an association was formed to help workers to develop their knowledge and skills to manufacture and operate machinery in the local mills. The organization held educational classes, offered educational scholarships, and even set up plans to aid widows, families, or disabled workers.

In 1857, the non-profit organization needed a building of its own; the Association's then president, Ichabod Washburn, a wire industrialist, hired Elbridge Boyden as designer and contractor. The building, Mechanics Hall, was to represent the newest mechanical systems and construction techniques.

By 1859, not only did the new building house industrial conventions, it was home to meetings for abolitionists to women's suffrage groups. The first - and the nation's oldest - music festival was also held there. In 1864, as the Civil War rumbled, the citizens of Worcester raised the money and asked the two brothers Elias and George Greenleaf Hook in Boston to build the four-keyboard organ. The organ has 3,504 pipes and

Mechanics Hall. *Cancelled Aug 16, 1910, as is $3-4*

52 stops and is the oldest unaltered organ in America. (It is currently in fine condition and was featured in the 1984 movie "The Bostonians"). The Hall became the cultural cornerstone of central Massachusetts before the Civil War of 1865. Mechanics Hall was not simply a concert hall. Henry David Thoreau, Ralph Waldo Emerson, Charles Dickens, and Mark Twain were among the authors who lectured there. The most successful of these early "mechanics" soon became inventors, entrepreneurs, and directors of large scale enterprises. They attained a social status equal to that of the earlier aristocrats and landed gentry.

By the 1950s, few organizations used the hall; to pay bills, the Association scheduled roller skating, basketball, and wrestling matches at the hall. Because of this, the interior was neglected and later, Worcester citizens raised five million dollars for its award-winning restoration in 1977. They refurbished the cast-iron facade, retained the graffiti from 1869 and the black walnut ticket kiosks with their elegant carvings and hand-etched glass windows, added ten period chandeliers, and also completed a portrait gallery of 19th century leaders. The largest room known as the Great Hall has a richly decorated coffered ceiling, Corinthian pilasters and balustrade balcony, and the largest hard-wood dance floor in New England.

Renovated once again in the twenty-first century Mechanics Hall is listed in the National Register of Historic Places and is one of the four finest concert halls in North America and one of the twelve finest in the world. To preserve this non-profit world-class Hall, the Association relies on income from Hall rentals for recordings of label companies like Telarc, Koch, and Sony; rentals for proms, graduations, benefit dinners and weddings; memberships and contributions; and revenue from the Hall's Gift Shop. The Hall's Gift Shop carries unusual gifts including Steinbach nutcrackers, Selkirk glass, and Pipka Santas.

The Hall's world class recording studio features two Steinway (New York/Hamburg) nine-foot concert grand pianos and the Hook organ. The superb sound system offers fine acoustics, reverberation time and low background noise level. In the past, classical artists including Yo-Yo Ma, The Cleveland Quartet, and James Taylor have made recordings in the Hall. Throughout Mechanics Hall history, Thoreau and Dickens, Caruso, Dvorak, Teddy Roosevelt and Elizabeth Cady Stanton, Itzak Perlman, Mel Torme and Ella Fitzgerald have performed at the Hall.

Mechanics Hall can accommodate 10 to 1600 people from world class events to intimate and exclusive weddings each planned with precise detail by the Associations professional Event Planner. The Hall is air conditioned, handicapped accessible and includes an assistive loop hearing system.

Working with Worcester Public Schools, sponsored by the Greater Worcester Community, Worcester Cultural Commission, and others, Mechanics Hall offers a free series of teacher workshops and brown bag lunch-time concerts for school-age children. And because the Association wants everyone in the community to enjoy the Hall, they offer tapes, videos, tours, and speakers to community, school or business groups - sharing the history of Mechanics Hall.

Worcester's EcoTarium is well rooted in the community as an organization dedicated to the study of science and nature. The private, non-profit institution was founded in 1825 as the Worcester Lyceum of Natural History and was incorporated in 1884 as the Worcester Natural History Society - EcoTarium's legal identity. The transition from the New England Science Center to the EcoTarium in 1998 refocused the museum on its roots in the natural sciences with a focus on hands-on exploration and discovery. The name change accompanied a major capital development program that has transformed the building and grounds into an accessible learning and discovery center for families.

Military Escort passing down Main Street, Train Men's Association Convention, Worcester, Mass., April 3, 1910. *Circa 1910, $8-9*

President Taft leaving Mechanics Hall, Worcester, MA, April 3, 1910. Copy of the original photographed used for the post card, *1910. $4-5*

In the late 1990s, the EcoTarium expansion projects opened previously unseen corners of the museum and grounds to visitors. Today, the museum has turned its focus to investing in new exhibits inside the museum building, exhibits that bring the wonder of science and nature to life. In addition, Worcester is home to the Higgins Armory Museum and the nation's only plumbing museum, the American Sanitary Plumbing Museum.

Chapter 5
Parks

In March of 1854, the city of Worcester purchased land and contracted Olmstead (of Central Park and Boston's Emerald Necklace fame) to design a park that would become Elm Park. It was the first time a city in the United States had acquired land for such a purpose.

Twenty-first-century photo of the ornate Iron Bridge at Elm Park.

Worcester, Mass., Elm Park.

Bridge over the pond in Elm Park. Currently the bridge is a wooden structure constructed in the 20th century. *Cancelled Aug 25, 1908, $4-5*

Boat House, Elm Park, Worcester, Mass.

Boat House, Elm Park, Worcester, Mass. *Cancelled Sep 4, 1913, $4-5*

Twenty-first-century photo of the bridge at Elm Park, near Park Avenue.

VIEW IN ELM PARK, WORCESTER, MASS.

View in Elm Park, Worcester, Mass. It was Worcester Park Commissioner: Edward Winslow Lincoln who ensured a park was built on the land purchased in 1854. The pond is man-made and the park was dedicated to the citizens of Worcester in 1905. *Cancelled Nov 23, 1908, $3-4*

Bancroft Tower, Worcester, Mass. The Bancroft Tower was erected to the memory of the Bancroft family of Worcester, Massachusetts. Aaron Bancroft was a revolutionary soldier, clergyman and author. His son, George (1800-1891) was born in Worcester. A distinguished historian and statesman, he established the Naval Academy at Annapolis when Secretary of the Navy under President Polk. He founded the Round Hill School at Northampton, the first serious effort in the U.S. to elevate secondary education to its rightful place. Built in 1900 by Stephen Salisbury III and bequeathed to the Worcester Art Museum; the Tower still stands today. *Cancelled Feb 2, 1910, $3-4*

Bancroft Tower on Bancoft Hill, Bancroft Monument, Rural Cemetry, Birthplace of George Bancroft. Card in honor of George Bancroft a Worcester Historian 1800-1891. Published by William A. Emerson, 8 Lincoln Ave., Worcester, Mass. "Emerson's Old-Time Souvenir Post Card" *Circa 1910, $5-6*

Bancroft Tower, photographed in 2008, looks almost exactly like the 1910 picture

Russell Street Entrance Elm Park, Worcester, Mass.

Russell Street Entrance to Elm Park. In 1854, Worcester was the first City in the U.S. to purchase land in order to preserve the natural environment and to provide a park for its residents. German card, *Circa 1900, $2-3*

The Oval, Worcester, Mass.

The Oval, near Lake Park, was opened in 1891 as the City's sporting facility. *Circa 1900s, $15-18*

Entrance Green Hill Park, WORCESTER, Mass.

Entrance Green Hill Park, Worcester, Mass. The largest park in Worcester with almost 500 acres and a 60 acre man-made pond. Turned over to the city in 1903 at the request of benefactor Andrew Haswell Green. *Cancelled Oct 7, 1910, $4-5*

Today, in cooperation with the Parks and Recreation Commissioner, the Commission is responsible for supervising the maintenance of 1200 acres of municipally owned park land, the operation of the city owned golf course, the provision of athletic facilities, tennis courts, basketball courts, etc. The Parks, Recreation and Cemetery Division is responsible for the operation of the city owned cemetery and is also responsible for the operation and maintenance of Worcester Common, City Hall and the Grand Army of the Republic (G.A.R.) Hall.

The Grand Army of the Republic (G.A.R.) began as an organization for Civil War discharged veterans of the Union Army, Navy, and the Marine Corps in 1866 for camaraderie. By 1890, more than 400,000 Union veterans had joined G.A.R. Posts. Today G.A.R. is an active organization with membership opened to men and women who can prove an ancestor fought for the Union.

In the early years of the G.A.R. organization, the Worcester Post bought the four-story Bull Mansion on Pearl Street residing there until the 1930s. No longer able to afford the building's maintenance, they transferred the G.A.R. building to the city. Government officials of the City of Worcester hired Lamoureux Pagano Associates (a creative Worcester architectural firm with projects ranging from the simple to the complex) to renovate the Grand Army of the Republic (G.A.R.) Hall.

In recent years, Mitchell Terricciano purchased the building, and after a two-million-dollar restoration, opened his high-end restaurant. In 2007, the restaurant went up for sale in a foreclosure auction. The property has 11, 295 square feet, a full kitchen with walk-in coolers and freezers, a dumbwaiter; many dining rooms, a bar and lounge; offices and a function room, a new elevator and is completely handicapped accessible. Currently, William Bibaud, a Worcester property owner, is collaborating with the members of Preservation Worcester to re-open this signature property.

Today, some of the many missions of the Department of Public Works and Parks is to maintain all 1,215 acres of city parks, playgrounds, beaches, and street trees, as well as maintaining the cemetery and public buildings - all with the goal to improve the quality of life for the citizens and visitors of Worcester.

GEO. H. WARD POST 10, G.A.R.
MEMORIAL BUILDING
WORCESTER, MASSACHUSETTS

COPYRIGHT, 1912, GEO. H. WARD, POST 10, G. A. R., WORCESTER, MASS.

BARROWS-STJERNLOF

Geo. H. Ward Post 10. G.A.R. Memorial Building, Worcester, Massachusetts, Copyright, 1912. Back Made In Worcester, Plates by Carlton Engraving Co., Printing by Geo. W. King & Sons. *Circa 1912, $12-15*

Tower, Greenwood Park, Worcester, Mass. *Circa 1900, $3-4*

Green Hill Park, General View, Worcester, Mass. Published by Perkins & Butler, Inc., Worcester, Mass. Today it has a large Vietnam Veteran's Memorial. *Circa 1910s, $3-4*

Worcester, Mass., Green Hill Park. Along the Shore. *Cancelled Aug 11, 1911, $3-4*

Playgrounds, Greenwood Park, Worcester, Mass.
Cancelled Jan 30, 1911, $2-3

Lake, Institute Park, Worcester, Mass. *Circa 1900s, $3-4*

Bridge and Walk, Institute Park, Worcester, Mass. *Cancelled Mar 31, 1911, $4-5*

INSTITUTE PARK, WORCESTER, MASS.

Institute Park, Worcester, Mass. Located across the street from WPI on Salisbury Street - between Salisbury and Grove Streets. Given to the City on October 1, 1887 by Stephen Salisbury III. *Circa 1900, $3-4*

Old Mill, Institute Park. Worcester, Mass.

Old Mill, Institute Park, Worcester, Mass. "Made in Germany for A.P.Lundborg, Publisher, Worcester, Mass. (13375)" *Circa 1910s, $10-11*

INSTITUTE PARK, WORCESTER, MASS.

Institute Park, Worcester, Mass. The park comprises approximately 18 acres. *Cancelled Jan 1, 1907, $3-4*

84

Worcester, Mass., Lincoln Park, Thule Club. *Cancelled Jul 5, 1910, $10-11*

University Park looking towards Clark University, Worcester, Mass.
Cancelled Oct 5, 1912, $8-9

University Park, Worcester, Mass.
Cancelled 4 Jun 1909, $3-4

Quinsigamond Lake, Worcester, Mass. "Just to let you know I'm living. Alice M. Perry" *Cancelled Jan 7, 1911, $3-4*

Wachusett Boat Club, Lake Quinsigamond, Worcester, Mass. *Cancelled Dec 24, 1906, $3-4*

Causeway bridge connecting the North and South ends, Lake Quinsigamond, Worcester, Mass. *Circa 1900, $4-5*

New Lake Quinsigamond Bridge, Worcester, Mass. "H.F. Davis, Photo" "New Lake Quinsigamond Bridge, finished 1919 and built by Samuel H. Pitcher Co., of Worcester, Massachusetts, at the cost of $325,000" *Cancelled Mar 20, 1920, $8-10*

Lincoln Park, Lake Quinsigamond, Worcester, Mass. *Circa 1900s, $4-5*

Lake Quinsigamond, Worcester, Mass. Embellished with glitter. *Cancelled Jul 21, 1906, $3-4*

North Park, Worcester, Mass. *Cancelled Jul 21, 1908, $5-6*

"Open-Air Theatre, Lake Quinsigamond, Worcster, Mass" Metropolitan News Co., Boston in red circle on front. *Circa 1900, $10-11*

Women's Bathing House, Lake Quinsigamond, Worcster, Mass. "Lake Quinsigamond, one of the most beautiful lakes in New England, is the principal pleasure resort of Worcster. On the Shores are situated the White City, Lakeside Park and many Clubhouses. For Boating, Bathing, Fishing, Skating and kindred Sports no better place can be found." *Cancelled Aug 29, 1917, $15-20*

The Grove, Pinehurst Park,
Worcester, Mass.
Cancelled May 9, 1908, $3-4

COES POND, WORCESTER, MASS.   O.K. My birthday. 1908
Lora.

Coes Pond, Worcester, Mass. "O.K. My birthday. Lora. 1908"
Cancelled Dec 19, 1907. $4-5

White City from Bridge, Worcester, Mass. *Cancelled Nov 2, 1940, $5-6*

Dance hall, White City, Worcester, Mass. Published by J.I.Williams, Worcester, Mass. *Circa 1900s, $10-15*

The White City, Worcester, Mass. *Cancelled Sep 8, 1909, $8-10*

The White City, Worcester, Mass. *Cancelled Apr 3, $3-4*

90

"The Worcester Science Center, Worcester, MA is a unique complex where all ages can discover the wonders of the natural sciences. The Center is composed of a three level museum building; planetarium; nature trails; outdoor live animal exhibits and a miniature railroad all set on the 60 acre grounds." Currently known as the EcoTarium. Card *Circa 1950s, $1-2*

King's Lane. Worcester, Mass. *Circa 1910s, $3-4*

Worcester Counties Mammoth Birch.
Circa 1910s, $2-3

Elephant Elm. Worcester, Mass.
Circa 1900s, $2-3

Chapter 6
Hospitals

Worcester has been on the cutting edge of treatment, healthcare and research since the first publicly-supported hospital in the United States was established in 1834 to treat mental illness and psychiatric disorders. The Worcester State Lunatic Hospital also known as the Bloomingdale Insane Hospital and later named the Worcester State Hospital and was a pioneer in treating mental illness as a disease. In 1909, Dr. Freud visited the Worcester State Hospital on his only visit to the United States of America. Dr. Samuel B. Woodward was the first superintendent and a leader in the research of psychiatry. Dr. Woodward was one of the founders and first president of what is known today as the American Psychiatric Association.

State Hospital for the Insane, Worcester, Mass. "I have been here - it is a city by itself. Goodby Teress" *Cancelled Aug 13, 1906 $8-9*

Birdseye View of Lincoln Park and Bloomingdale Insane Hospital, Worcester, Mass. Bloomingdale Insane Hospital later known as Worcester State Hospital. *Cancelled Nov 8, 1913, $8-9*

State Hospital, Worcester, Mass. A pioneer in treating mental illness as a disease. *Circa 1900s, $9-10*

Noted for firsts, the medical field is also represented. In 1960, the first birth control pill was approved by FDA, and it was developed at the Worcester Foundation for Experimental Biology, located near Shrewsbury. And the Cambridge Biotech Corporation in Worcester received a federal license for the first HIV diagnostic test.

There are a number of major medical facilities located in Worcester today including the University of Massachusetts (UMass) Medical School, located on Lake Avenue. It is ranked fourth in primary care education among America's top 125 medical schools and is number one in research and community service. The school operates the University of Massachusetts (UMass) Memorial Health Care (which incorporated UMass Medical Hospital) and has expanded not only in Worcester but all around the state. The University of Massachusetts Medical School and UMass Memorial Health Care, Inc., are the number one and number two employers in Worcester.

Hahnemann Hospital, Lincoln Street, Worcester, Mass. The former mansion of the Roche estate remodeled and opened in 1909. *Circa 1910, $8-9*

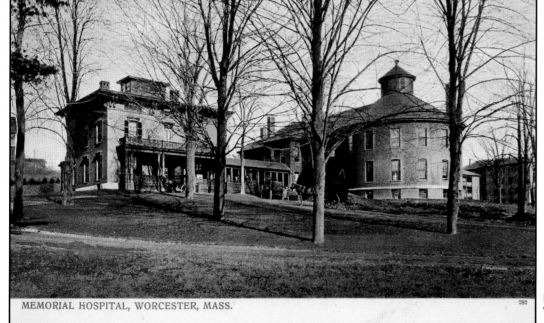

MEMORIAL HOSPITAL, WORCESTER, MASS.

The U-Mass Medical School, established in 1962, is home to the Lamar Soutter Library (named for the University's first dean Dr. Lamar Soutter) a world class reference library staffed with experts in every field to assist medical researchers. Aware of the historic importance of the University of Massachusetts Medical School, Dr. Ellen S. More was hired as the first head of the office of Medical Historian and Archives.

Craig Mello, Nobel Laureate, is the 2006 Nobel Prize winner for physiology and medicine.

Memorial Hospital, Worcester, Mass. A bequest by Ichabod Washburn, Washburn and Moen Manufacturing Company, in honor of his two daughters. Opened in June 1888 original to treat just women and children. Nothing is left of Memorial Hospital as shown. *Circa 1900, $8-9*

94

Doctors Hospital of Worcester, Lincoln Street. Doctors Hospital is a fully accredited hospital of 121 beds and is a short-term general hospital. *Circa 1968s, $2-3*

"City Hospital, Memorial Home for Nurses. Worcester, Mass." Published by the Jones Supply Co., Worcester, Mass. *$8-9*

City Hospital. This hospital is no longer. *Circa 1900s, $8-9*

WORCESTER CITY HOSPITAL, WORCESTER, MASS.

WINSLOW SURGERY, CITY HOSPITAL, WORCESTER, MASS.

"Worcester City Hospital, Worcester, Mass., situated on Jacques Ave., was incorporated in 1871 and is under the management of trustees chosen by the city. The hospital has received from the estate of George Jacques and from the gifts and bequests of many other citizens, a sum amounting to over $500,000. It also has a training school for nurses." *Cancelled May 18, 1916, $5-6*

Winslow Surgery Building, City Hospital, Worcester, MASS. *Circa 1900, $8-9*

"Worcester City Hospital (Reconstruction), Jaques Ave., Worcester, Mass. Pleasand 6-1551. Unusual, "pin-wheel" hospital design. Beautiful sunny rooms with every modern convenience. Extensive views over the City. Most modern equipment and facilities for your doctor to work with. Isadore & Zachary Rosen field & E. Todd Wheeler - Architects, Dr. Albert W. Snoke - Consultant, Theodore A. Austin - Superintendent. *Circa 1940s, $2-3*

Damaged Post Card with Historical Value of Nurses' Home, Worcester State Hospital, Worcester, Mass. *Cancelled Oct 16, 1911, $1-2*

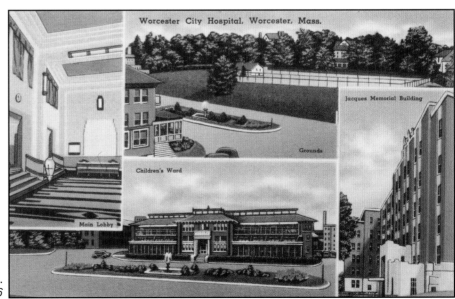

1942 Overview of updated Worcester City Hospital.
Circa 1940s, $5-6

St Vincent Hospital is currently located in downtown near the DCU Center and focuses on primary care. Fallon Clinic was the creator of Fallon Community Health Plan (HMO) one of the largest health maintenance organizations in the state. Fairlawn Rehab and Outpatient and near-by Hubbard Regional Hospital currently take care of the many Worcester residents.

St Vincent Hospital, Worcester, Mass. Opened in 1893.
Circa 1900, $6-7

ST. VINCENT HOSPITAL, WORCESTER, MASS.

St Vincent Hospital, Worcester, Mass., Cancelled Feb 5, 1932, with "Worcester We Aim At Excellence." *$3-4*

98

Another view of St Vincent Hospital. *Circa 1930s, $4-5*

ST. VINCENT HOSPITAL. WORCESTER. MASS.

"The "new" 650 bed St Vincent Hospital, Worcester, Mass. Largest private hospital in central Ma, has dominated the skyline of Worcester since its dedication in April 1954. Modern Clinics and Research bring up to date the healing arts under the direction of the Sisters of Providence. *Circa 1960s, $2-3*

Chapter 7
Education

Worcester has evolved into an education, medical and research center with thirteen colleges and universities and five hospitals. Worcester is home of the oldest Catholic college in the United States the College of the Holy Cross founded in 1843. Billy Collins, former Poet Laureate, Bob Cousy, and Supreme Court Justice Clarence Thomas all graduated from Holy Cross. It was ranked as the 32nd highest liberal arts college in 2007.

Holy Cross College, Worcester, Mass.
Circa 1940s, $3-4

Holy Cross College,
O'Kane Hall,
Worcester, Mass,
Circa 1910s, $3-4

Base Ball Field, Holy Cross College, Worcester, Mass. *Circa 1900s, $20-25*

Worcester, Mass, Fitton Avenue, Holy Cross College. Embellished with glitter, ca., *1910s $3-4*

Alumni Hall (under construction)
Holy Cross, Worcester, Mass.
Cancelled Nov 24, 1907, $3-4

Twenty-first century photo of the original clock at the College of the Holy Cross.

Twenty-first-century photo of the entrance to the College of the Holy Cross.

Worcester Polytechnic Institute (better known as WPI) was founded twenty years later in 1865 and continues to be a leader in biotechnology and engineering education. Clark University founded in 1887 offers psychology and geography studies and an exclusive PhD study in Holocaust History and Genocide Studies. Past professors include Nobel Prize Winner of 1902 Albert Michelson, the God Father of the space age Robert Goddard, and the founder of American Psychological Association and organizer of psychology as a science G. Stanley Hall.

Worcester Polytechnic Institute Worcester, Mass. Alden Memorial Auditorium, Sanford Riley Hall, Electrical Engineering Building, Higgins Mechanical Engineering Laboratories. *Cancelled May 9, 1946, $3-4*

Worcester Polytechnic Institute, Worcester, Mass. *Circa 1910, $3-4*

Polytechnic Institute, Worcester, Mass. "Illustrated Post Card Co., N.Y."
Circa 1900s, $4-5

Worcester, Mass., Polytechnic Institute, Salisbury Laboratories. *Circa 1900s, $4-5*

Boynton Hall, Mechanical Lab and Foundry at Worcester Polytechnic Institute.
Worcester, Mass. *Cancelled Feb 9, 1912, $3-4*

Twenty-first-century photo of Worcester Polytechnic Iinstitute entrance on Salisbury
Street.

104

Clark University Founded 1887. At the south end of Main Street is an institution of scientific research. The Clark University sign introduces the ivy covered Library building with the world-famous Geography building adjacent to it.
Cancelled Sep 4, 1963, $1-2

"Clark University Founded 1887. At the south end of Main Street is an institution of scientific research. Dr. G. Stanley Hall is the President of the University." *$3-4*

Clark University, Worcester, Mass.
Alumni Gymnasium, Jonas G.
Clark Hall, Atwood Hall and Library.
Cancelled Jul 8, 1952, $3-4

Library, Clark's University, Worcester, MASS. *Cancelled Aug 27, 1913, $3-4*

Clark University rare hold to light post card made in Germany for A.P. Lundborg, Worcester, Mass. *Cancelled Sep 4, 1901, $20-25*

Assumption College Chapel of the Holy Spirit. "A cruciform structure incorporates the age-old form in a contemporary building." *Circa 1960s, $3-4*

Assumption College, founded in 1904, is the fourth oldest Catholic college in New England. The campus is located on 175 acres - the largest campus in Worcester. Worcester State College was named the best NE college in 2005-8 by the Princeton Review.

French House of Assumption College. *Circa 1950s, $3-4*

Assumption College, Salisbury Street was founded in 1904 and destroyed by a tornado in 1953 has been (was) rebuilt at this new Salisbury Street site. A liberal arts College, Assumption specializes in modern languages and foreign affairs. Masters programs are offered in languages, psychology & guidance, social studies, education and fine arts. *Circa 1950s, $3-4*

LA GROTTE, THE GROTTO. ASSUMPTION COLLEGE, WORCESTER, MASS.

La Grotte, The Grotto, Assumption College, Worcester, MASS.
Cancelled Sep 14, 19??, $3-4

Ave Maria College, founded in 1946 was recently named the safest college community in the nation in a national survey. Salter College is a private school specializing in business and computer education. Becker College founded in 1784 offers associate, bachelor degrees, and adult learning degrees.

Office of Becker's Business College, 98 Front St., Worcester, Mass.

Office of Becker's Business College, 98 Front Street, Worcester, Mass.
Cancelled Aug, 1912, $5-6

Quinsigamond Community College offers forty associate degrees and certificate studies. Oread Institute, the first woman's college was founded in Worcester in 1849 by Eli Thayer, and was modeled after a program offered at Brown University, where Eli had attended school. Laura Spelman (John D. Rockefeller's future wife) attended Oread. Spelman college was later opened in her name, and abolitionist John Brown was an instructor there. Oread college closed in 1898. The Worcester Domestic Science Cooking School continued to use the Oread Institute campus through 1904. It closed its doors in 1934.

The University of Massachusetts Medical School, founded in 1970, continues to be one of the top fifty medical schools in the nation, ranking fourth out of 125 medical schools for primary care education. Tufts University Veterinary School was the first college/university to offer a four-year doctor of veterinary medicine with a master of public health degree (DVM and MPH) and continues to pioneer in veterinary ethics.

The Massachusetts College of Pharmacy and Health Sciences, located on 25 Foster Street the site of the vacant Albert Spencer Lowell Building, opened a campus in Worcester in 2000. Due to the leadership and innovated thinking of the current President - Charles Monahan - the "legacy of excellence" continues at Massachusetts College of Pharmacy and Health Sciences. It was President Monahan's creative thinking, business savvy, intimate understanding of the College and his promise to help alleviate the shortage of pharmacists in the U.S. that broadened the College's boundaries from Boston to a campus in Manchester, New Hampshire and to his hometown Worcester, Massachusetts.

Collaborating with the Colleges of Worcester Consortium, President Monahan has launched several community service programs in Worcester to include an innovative nursing program with St. Vincent's and Worcester Medical Center. "To date, the College has invested more than $44 million in the future of Worcester and its role as a center for health care delivery," said President Monahan. Providing partnerships all over the world with a sincere commitment to caring - President Charles Monahan (an Isaiah Thomas Award winner) is a true Worcester living legend.

As a note, Lamoureux Pagano Associates, Worcester, MA (a creative architectural firm with projects ranging from the simple to the complex) combines art with science. The firm was honored in 2007 as a winner of the first School Building Design Awards, sponsored by the Massachusetts School Building Authority and State Treasurer Timothy Cahill. The awards recognize school building design successes and serve to identify model elements of existing buildings to help inform the Authority's new school building regulations.

One of the schools that Lamoureux renovated was the Worcester Technical High School. Hired by the city to enhance the learning environment for 1500 students, the 390,000 square foot school is divided into four clusters: Manufacturing Technologies, Business Management, Health and Human Services, and Construction Technologies. Each cluster is organized in direct association with academic classrooms. The entire school is equipped with state-of-the-art features including wireless technologies.

Lamoureux also renovated Worcester's Quinsigamond School. Honored by the Massachusetts Historical Commission, the new pre-kindergarten through sixth grade school occupies an entire city block. New construction joins the existing Quinsigamond School (constructed in 1890) with the Quinsigamond Public Library (constructed in 1913). Mr. Neil Collins, then Construction Coordinator for Worcester Public Schools, stated, "Quinsigamond School is a perfect blend of historic preservation and new construction that serves as the jewel of this south Worcester neighborhood. The students, teachers, and parents are appreciative of the wonderful opportunities found within this beautiful school."

Oread Institute, Worcester, Mass.

Oread Institute, Worcester, Mass. *Cancelled Sep 27, 1912, $3-4*

Trade School, Worcester, Mass.

Trade School, Worcester, Mass.
Cancelled July 12, 1917, $3-4

Twenty-first-century photo of Technical High School, that sits abandoned in downtown. The new High School is located off Green Street.

110

"Worcester Academy's New Gymnasium, completed and dedicated November 13, 1915; costs $100,000 and is considered the best preparatory school athletic nome in New England. Its swimming pool, 75 feet long by 30 feet wide, will mark the beginning of world activity in swimming at the school. The new chapel completes the wall of buildings around the campus. *Cancelled Jul 14, 1921, $3-4*

Adams Hall, Worcester Academy, *Circa 1900, $3-4*

Walker Hall, Worcester Academy, *Cancelled Aug 16, 1911, $4-5*

Worcester Academy Buildings.
Circa 1900s, $3-4

WORCESTER ACADEMY BUILDINGS, WORCESTER, MASS.

Worcester Academy, Worcester, Mass. *Circa 1900, $4-5*

Bancroft School, Worcester, Mass. Published by J.I. Williams, Worcester, Mass Circle around a heart states: "In Worcester We Aim at Excellence Write It On Your Heart" *Circa 1900s, $6-7*

Highland Military Academy, Worcester, Mass. *Circa 1900, $3-4*

High School, Elm & Water Sts., Worcester, Mass. *Circa 1900s, $3-4*

High School, Worcester, Mass. "July 1.1907 Clinton" *Cancelled Jul 1, 1907, $2-3*

Classical High School and English High School. *Circa 1900s, $4-5*

English High School, Worcester, Mass. *Circa 1900s, $4-5*

Tatnuck School, Worcester, Mass.

05576-PUBLISHED BY E B. LUCE

Tatnuck School, Worcester, Mass.
Cancelled Mar 21, 1913, $2-3

South High School, Worcester
Mass. Embellished with glitter.
Circa 1910, $4-5

673   SOUTH HIGH SCHOOL, WORCESTER, MASS.   ILLUST. POST CARD CO., N. Y.

Chapter 8
Sacred Places

In the beginning, Worcester had three churches: the Old South Meeting House, the First Unitarian Church and St. John's Roman Catholic Church. Today there are more than eight hundred denominations, more than a hundred religious organizations, and more than two hundred places to worship in the Worcester area– each with unique building styles, interior divisions, and architectural elements.

Worcester's first church—the Old South Church —just a log cabin in 1717, became the first frame church in 1719, and the second frame church in 1763. Demolished in 1887 to make way for the City Hall (there is currently a bronze star in the sidewalk where the church once sat) it was reconstructed by its congregation in 1889 and became known as the Old South Congregational located at Main and Wellington Streets. After 1879 the building was made into residential housing.

A disgruntled group of members of the Old South Church split and in 1792 the First Unitarian Church was formed and became the second church in Worcester. Reconstructed in 1829 at 90 Main Street, it burnt to the ground in 1849 and was rebuilt in 1851. Once again destroyed in 1938 (by the famous 1938 New England hurricane) it was rebuilt to the exact replication of the original and stands in the exact location today.

Worcester, Mass., Old South Church, Log Cabin Church 1717, First Frame Church 1719, Second Frame Church 1763, this Building completed 1889.
Cancelled Mar 9, 1910, $3-4

Worcester, Mass., Old South Church, Log Cabin Church 1717, First Frame Church 1719, Second Frame Church 1763, this Building completed 1889.

116

Unitarian Church in Ruins at Worcester, Mass.

THE GREAT NEW ENGLAND HURRICANE OF 1938

PHOTO BY INT. NEWS SERVICE

Unitarian Church in Ruins at Worcester, Mass. The Great New England Hurricane of 1938. September 21, 1938, will long be remembered as the date of the Big Hurricane which swept New England -- in all history something never before known to this part of the country. The loss of lives was appalling; property damage mounted to hundreds of millions of dollars and the homeless counted to hundreds of thousands. The tremendous fury of the wind left behind destruction, destitution and utter ruin. *Circa 1938, $9-10*

MAIN STREET, UNITARIAN CHURCH AND WESLEY CHURCH BEYOND, WORCESTER, MASS.

63326

Main Street, Unitarian Church and Wesley Church beyond, Worcester, Mass. *Cancelled Aug 8, 1942, $3-4*

Twenty-first-century photograph of the Wesley and Unitarian Church on Main Street.

Wesley Church on Main Street.

St. John's Roman Catholic Church was built in 1845 and moved in 1846 to its present location at 44 Temple Street. There was an addition added in 1884 and the church is the oldest religious structure in Worcester today. In May, 2008 the Bishop of Worcester, Reverend Robert J. McManus, announced the decision for Worcester parish reconfiguration. This was based on low offertory support in relation to the number of registered Catholic households and the high number of (29) operating parishes. Based on the information from focus groups and interviews, the bishop announced that four parishes be closed and merged with other parishes: Holy Name of Jesus Parish, St. Casimir Parish, Ascension Parish, and St. Margaret Mary Parish. Additionally, Notre Dame des Canadiens Church building will be closed. He noted in his letter the he has "become convinced for pastoral reasons such as declining Mass attendance and little or no religious education or sacramental life that the spiritual lives of the parishioners would be better served in parishes with a more vibrant pastoral."

St. Ann Orphanage Grotto, Worcester, Mass. *Cancelled Jun 21, 1944, $2-3*

The First Baptist Church of Worcester, Mass., situated on Salisbury Street at Park Ave., opposite Institute Park and adjoining the Campus of the Worcester Polytechnic Institute. Organized Dec 9, 1812, the present building was dedicated Sept 24, 1939. *Circa 1950s, $1-2*

New Baptist Church, Worcester, Mass. *Circa 1910s, $3-4*

First Church of Christ Scientist, Worcester, Mass. *Cancelled Nov 2, 1914, $4-5*

Interior, Notre Dame Church, Worcester, Mass. *Circa 1900s, $5-6*

Notre Dame Des Canadiens, Salem Square, Worcester, Mass.
(Formerly the First Baptist Church). Note: In May 2008 the diocese
placed this church on the closure list. *Cancelled Sep 14, 1910, $3-4*

St. Annes Church, Worcester, Mass.
Circa 1900, $3-4

Masonic Temple, Worcester, Mass. *Cancelled May 25, 1916, $3-4*

Worcester, Mass, St. Anne's Catholic Church. *Cancelled Aug 14, 1911, $2-3*

121

St Paul's Church, Worcester, Mass. *Cancelled Oct 30, 1923. $3-4*

Interior of St. Paul's Church. *Circa 1900s, $4-5*

St. Paul's Church, Worcester, Mass. *"Sept 6, 1947," $3-4*

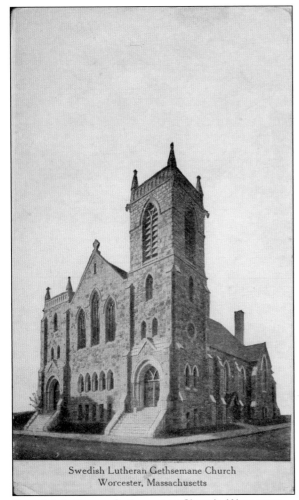

Swedish Lutheran Gethsemane Church, Worcester, Massachusetts. Made in Worcester by Pearson The Printer. *Circa 1910s, $4-5*

Trinity Church, Worcester, Mass. *Circa 1900s, $3-4*

St. Peter's Catholic Church, 935 Main Street, Worcester, Mass. *Circa 1900s, $4-5*

CHAPEL, HOPE CEMETERY, WORCESTER, MASS.

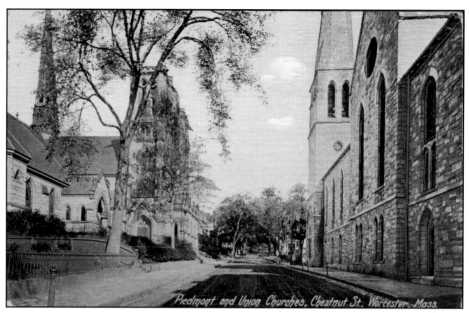

Piedmont and Union Churches, Chestnut St., Worcester, Mass.
Cancelled Sep 12, 1916, $4-5

Union Church, Worcester, Mass. *Cancelled Jul 28, 1911, $3-4*

Chapel, Hope Cemetery, Worcester, Mass. *Circa 1900s, $3-4*

Wesley Methodist Church, Main Street near Lincoln Square Worcester, Massachusetts. New England's largest Protestant Church. Gothic architecture - Cathedral windows depict history of Christian faith. Chapel open daily for prayer. *Circa 1920s, $3-4*

Twenty-first-century photo of Union Congregational Church on Chestnut Street, minus the original steeple.

Twenty-first-century photo of The United Congregational Church, at 6 Institute Road, with the Armory on Salisbury Street in the background.

Twenty-first-century photo of the beautiful, park-like cemetery on Grove Street.

Chapter 9

Worcester's Historical Museum

Worcester's Historical Museum (WHM) was founded in 1875 and is a "unique organization dedicated to collecting, preserving, interpreting Worcester's history in all time periods and subject areas." Many of the published works used in research of this book were provided by the Worcester Historical Museum. Membership is thirty dollars for an individual, forty dollars for a family and they offer student and senior citizen discounts. The following comes directly from their web site: Worcesterhistory.org

Worcester Historical Museum (WHM) is the only institution devoted to local history. It includes a research library of over 7,000 titles, an archive that houses thousands of documents, and a collection of artifacts, all vital to the study of Worcester history. A few examples of WHM's holdings include correspondence of abolitionist Abby Kelley Foster, Blackstone Canal Company records, Civil War era diaries and letters, and artifacts related to Worcester's industrial past including early woodenware and ceramics, weaponry from the colonial era through World War II, paintings and sculptures, and a significant costume and textile collection.

WHM also owns and operates the Salisbury Museum, Worcester's only historic house museum. Built in 1772, it has been restored to its 1830s appearance and one of the best documented historic houses in New England. Thanks to the voluminous family papers, preserved at the American Antiquarian Society, it is one of the best documented historic houses in New England.

Chapter 10
Preservation Worcester

Preservation Worcester is the only organization in the city dedicated to historic preservation. Established more than thirty years ago as a private not-for-profit membership organization, Preservation Worcester is dedicated to the preservation of Worcester's buildings, sites and neighborhoods. The organization was established in 1969 in response to urban renewal. At that time a large number of buildings were being demolished to make way for new buildings. They believe that these sites and buildings represent Worcester's history, culture and architecture and that by protecting these sites they are promoting community pride and identity. To further their goals, Preservation Worcester collaborates with state government, city officials, historical commissions, local colleges, developers, and neighborhood groups all the while "encouraging excellence in (future) design." A large part of Preservation Worcester's mission is education, including school and adult programs and walking and bus tours.

The following information has been taken directly off of the Preservation Worcester website: www.preservationworcester.org

For (the past) fourteen years, Preservation Worcester has published an annual list of Most Endangered Structures, with the goal of publicizing and alerting the public about the threats to some of our city's most historic buildings and sites. The List garners city-wide attention to the condition of these structures and their importance to our city. It often serves as a catalyst for restoration and preservation.

Over the years, the citizens and community leaders of Worcester have often responded with concern and aid, and important historic structures have been saved from the wrecking ball or demolition by neglect. Among the "success stories" from previous Most Endangered lists are: Bull Mansion/GAR Hall on Pearl Street, which was restored as a restaurant; the Chestnut Street Congregational Church, now the New England Dream Center; the Shaarai Torah Synagogue, recently converted into condos and lofts; the Rogers Kennedy Memorial in Elm Park which has been restored and rededicated; the Tiffany stained glass windows of St. Matthew's Episcopal Church on Southbridge Street near Holy Cross; the Quinsigamond Baptist Church, which was moved a quarter mile in Quinsigamond Village and is now the Steeple Marketplace; and the Worcester Five Cents Savings Bank Street Clock at 50 Front Street. The popular clock, erected in 1891, has been restored and is back in working order for the first time in many years.

Preservation Worcester's membership is forty dollars for an individual and sixty for a household. Preservation Worcester is responsible for the publication of many documents used as reference in this book and the organization continues to be dedicated to Worcester's historic preservation!

Twenty-first-century photo of The Fire Alarm and Telegraph Building on Park Avenue, currently on Preservation Worcester's endangered list.

Index